JOHNNY CASH

★ ★ ★ ★ ★ ★ ★ ★ ★ ★ ★ ★ ★ ★ ★

POP CULTURE LEGENDS

JOHNNY CASH

★ ★

SEAN DOLAN

CHELSEA HOUSE PUBLISHERS

New York ★ Philadelphia

CHELSEA HOUSE PUBLISHERS

EDITORIAL DIRECTOR   Richard Rennert
EXECUTIVE MANAGING EDITOR   Karyn Gullen Browne
COPY CHIEF   Robin James
PICTURE EDITOR   Adrian G. Allen
ART DIRECTOR   Robert Mitchell
MANUFACTURING DIRECTOR   Gerald Levine

Pop Culture Legends

SENIOR EDITOR   Kathy Kuhtz Campbell
SERIES DESIGN   Basia Niemczyc

Staff for JOHNNY CASH

EDITORIAL ASSISTANT   Kelsey Goss
DESIGN ASSISTANT   Lydia Rivera
PICTURE RESEARCHER   Wendy P. Wills
COVER ILLUSTRATION   Alan Reingold

The lyrics to "The Man in Black" are reprinted with permission. © 1971 by SONG OF CASH, INC. (ASCAP)

First Printing

1 3 5 7 9 8 6 4 2

Library of Congress Cataloging-in-Publication Data

Dolan, Sean.
Johnny Cash / Sean Dolan.
p. cm.—(Pop culture legends)
Includes bibliographical references and index.
ISBN 0-7910-2328-1.
    0-7910-2353-2 (pbk.)
1. Cash, Johnny—Juvenile literature. 2. Country musicians—United States—Biography—Juvenile literature. [1. Cash, Johnny. 2. Musicians. 3. Country music.] I. Title. II. Series.
ML3930.C27D64 1994   94-5141
782.42'1642'092—dc20   CIP
[B]   AC MN

FRONTISPIECE:
Timeless and essential, Johnny Cash's voice, presence, and songs have created a classic American legend.

Contents ★

A Reflection of Ourselves

Leeza Gibbons

I ENJOY A RARE PERSPECTIVE on the entertainment industry. From my window on popular culture, I can see all that sizzles and excites. I have interviewed legends who have left us, such as Bette Davis and Sammy Davis, Jr., and have brushed shoulders with the names who have caused a commotion with their sheer outrageousness, like Boy George and Madonna. Whether it's by nature or by design, pop icons generate interest, and I think they are a mirror of who we are at any given time.

Who are *your* heroes and heroines, the people you most admire? Outside of your own family and friends, to whom do you look for inspiration and guidance, as examples of the type of person you would like to be as an adult? How do we decide who will be the most popular and influential members of our society?

You may be surprised by your answers. According to recent polls, you will probably respond much differently than your parents or grandparents did to the same questions at the same age. Increasingly, world leaders such as Winston Churchill, John F. Kennedy, Franklin D. Roosevelt, and evangelist Billy Graham have been replaced by entertainers, athletes, and popular artists as the individuals whom young people most respect and admire. In surveys taken during each of the past 15 years, for example, General Norman Schwarzkopf was the only world leader chosen as the number one hero among high school students. Other names on the elite list joined by General Schwarzkopf included Paula Abdul, Michael Jackson, Michael Jordan, Eddie Murphy, Burt Reynolds, and Sylvester Stallone.

7

More than 30 years have passed since Canadian sociologist Marshall McLuhan first taught us the huge impact that the electronic media has had on how we think, learn, and understand—as well as how we choose our heroes. In the 1960s, Pop artist Andy Warhol predicted that there would soon come a time when every American would be famous for 15 minutes. But if it is easier today to achieve Warhol's 15 minutes of fame, it is also much harder to hold on to it. Reputations are often ruined as quickly as they are made.

And yet, there remain those artists and performers who continue to inspire and instruct us in spite of changes in world events, media technology, or popular tastes. Even in a society as fickle and fast moving as our own, there are still those performers whose work and reputation endure, pop culture legends who inspire an almost religious devotion from their fans.

Why do the works and personalities of some artists continue to fascinate us while others are so quickly forgotten? What, if any, qualities do they share that enable them to have such power over our lives? There are no easy answers to these questions. The artists and entertainers profiled in this series often have little more in common than the enormous influence that each of them has had on our lives.

Some offer us an escape. Artists such as actress Marilyn Monroe, comedian Groucho Marx, and writer Stephen King have used glamour, humor, or fantasy to help us escape from our everyday lives. Others present us with images that are all too recognizable. The uncompromising realism of actor and director Charlie Chaplin and folksinger Bob Dylan challenges us to confront and change the things in our world that most disturb us.

Some offer us friendly, reassuring experiences. The work of animator Walt Disney and late-night talk show host Johnny Carson, for example, provides us with a sense of security and continuity in a changing world. Others shake us up. The best work of composer John Lennon and actor James Dean will always inspire their fans to question and reevaluate the world in which they live.

It is also hard to predict the kind of life that a pop culture legend will lead, or how he or she will react to fame. Popular singers Michael Jackson

and Prince carefully guard their personal lives from public view. Other performers, such as popular singer Madonna, enjoy putting their private lives before the public eye.

What these artists and entertainers do share, however, is the rare ability to capture and hold the public's imagination in a world dominated by mass media and disposable celebrity. In spite of their differences, each of them has somehow managed to achieve legendary status in a popular culture that values novelty and change.

The books in this series examine the lives and careers of these and other pop culture legends, and the society that places such great value on their work. Each book considers the extraordinary talent, the stubborn commitment, and the great personal sacrifice required to create work of enduring quality and influence in today's world.

As you read these books, ask yourself the following questions: How are the careers of these individuals shaped by their society? What role do they play in shaping the world? And what is it that so captivates us about their lives, their work, or the images they present?

Hopefully, by studying the lives and achievements of these pop culture legends, we will learn more about ourselves.

The Man in Black

THE MAN IN BLACK onstage was tall and husky, with a face that could not be mistaken for anything other than American. As he had grown older and put behind him the craziness and hard times that had etched so many lines across it, that face had filled out, like the rest of him—his once-emaciated frame, laid waste by excess, sleeplessness, and fatigue, now effortlessly carried more than 200 pounds on its 74 inches—and even attained a kind of rugged handsomeness. But it still looked, as his admiring wife once put it, "lived in," showing every one of the long and hard miles he had traveled.

Deep-set dark eyes flashed above the high cheekbones that bespoke Native American ancestry; the left one, weakened by a childhood illness, tended to drift or droop a little. His nose was long and flaring and sat somewhat crookedly, its contours having been rearranged in one of the motor vehicle accidents that marked the bygone years of recklessness and darkness; scars adorned his right cheek also. When not hidden as now by his thick, backswept, gray-streaked black hair, which fell over the back of his collar, his ears protruded slightly; his thin-lipped mouth made him appear grim or

Johnny Cash's distinctive, deep bass voice is most often raised against a plain accompaniment of strummed acoustic guitar, electric guitar played as a rhythm instrument, bass, and drums, to an unvarying beat Cash once characterized as "boom-chicka-boom."

sad in repose. Though not infrequent, those grins that did crease his countenance seemed, though certainly not insincere, something of an aberration in a nature essentially more somber. One suspected that, like other melancholy characters, he welcomed laughter as a relief from the weighty, solitary concerns that were his constant companions, and placed a much higher value on it than did those whom it visited more often. Yet all the visible claims that experience had made on him were no more than equal to the attributes given him by legend; it was said that the scars were the result of a gunshot wound or a knife fight and that the hard edges of his character had been formed during long stints in jail, and there swirled about him the mysterious aura of the loner.

For all the extra flesh, which made him look not heavy but solid, rooted, like an old, gnarled, but seemingly unconquerable oak, there was yet—as one is still able to see, decades later, the physical characteristics of the child in the grown adult—something gaunt about him, a lean, hungry look coupled with a wiry strength that was peculiarly American and common to the people he came from:

In 1886 a family of immigrants pose before their covered wagon during their trek across Nebraska. Cash's ancestors were pioneers of Irish, Scottish, and English descent who traversed the Appalachians and settled on the Great Plains, near the Mississippi River.

the poor white farmers, most of them of Scottish, Irish, or English ancestry, who, in search of land, dignity, and freedom, had pushed the frontiers of the original 13 colonies away from the eastern seaboard, across the Appalachians, and on west to the big river, the Mississippi. When the night came, bringing with it an end to their labor picking cotton or digging coal from the stony, ungenerous land or milling timber from the huge forests that fell with their advance, they relaxed with banjos, fiddles, guitars, and mandolins, joining in high, lonesome harmonies on old ballads and hymns to a God they called merciful but who taught

His lessons through hardship and suffering. And they made up new songs, often to the old tunes, songs about horses, railroads, land, Judgment Day, family, hard times, whiskey, courtship, marriage, adultery, separation, murder, war, prison, rambling, damnation, home, salvation, and death.

A family of migrant farmers is photographed in a migrant camp in California during the height of the Great Depression. Formerly tenant farmers in Texas, this family was forced to move west to survive, in this case, picking peaches in Maryville, California.

Pushing onward, the descendants of these settlers and pioneers crossed the big river and claimed homesteads on the thin topsoil of the Great Plains, only to be blown away in the Great Depression when too many years of drought and hard use turned the Midwest into the Dust Bowl. These were the sharecroppers and tenant farmers photographed in the 1930s by Dorothea Lange and Walker Evans and memorialized in American literature by James Agee in *Let Us Now Praise Famous Men* and John Steinbeck in *The Grapes of Wrath:* used-up men and women in denim overalls and slouch hats and plain, faded cotton dresses, a few sticks of rude wooden furniture, a mattress, busted cardboard suitcases, and all their other earthly possessions piled high in the back of their Model T trucks. The men all seemed much older than their years, with seamed, leathery faces, their sunken cheeks covered with whiskery stubble, staring straight forward with unexpectant eyes; the women were resigned and careworn, surrounded by too many tousle-haired, dead-eyed children—all of them placing their hope, as always, in Jesus and in a promised land called California. Evicted by the wind and the dust and the unforgiving banks and landlords that held their mortgages and leases, tens of thousands of these "Okies" and "Arkies" migrated west during the 1930s, only to find in California a new kind of bondage to the land, as migrant workers in the Golden State's rich agricultural valleys.

They brought with them their music, enriched now by songs of the Old West, gunfighters, and the trail, but informed, as always, by the knowledge of hard times and the harder promise of deliverance, if only by death. Sung to the plaintive accompaniment of guitars, banjos, fiddles, occasionally a mandolin or a bass or a piano but never drums, called "hillbilly" and more respectfully "country," it was blasted far into the hinterlands from powerful radio stations just across the border in Mexico. After World War II it moved north as well with the country people who traveled to cities like Detroit, Michigan, and Gary, Indiana, to find work in the automobile plants, steel mills, and factories that were fueling victorious America's new prosperity. To a large extent, "working for the man" on an assembly line replaced picking cotton under a hot sun, but it was still

In the early 1930s, the Helton brothers play a fiddle and banjo duet, probably a fast, intricate tune from the hill country of the Carolinas. Because of its portability and simple construction, the fiddle became the most popular instrument in rural areas; the banjo, originally an African instrument brought to America by slaves, became prevalent with rural white musicians by the mid-19th century.

work, and the music was still country, though record company executives and disc jockeys came to prefer the tonier appellation "country and western."

The day-to-day experience of those who had lived these often forgotten or overlooked chapters in American history survived in the hollows and crags of the sad, stoic, and kind face of the tall man on the stage, and especially in the songs he had been singing for so many years. He wore a long, black swallow-tailed preacher's coat over a high-collared black shirt; his pants, too, and even his boots were black. With his back to the audience he strummed his old Martin guitar a couple of times, checking its tone, nodded to his longtime sidemen, and in the instant that the spotlight flared upon him, turned to the audience and spoke. "Hello," he said, "I'm Johnny Cash."

The voice, too, was lived-in. Unmistakably country, it yet lacked the nasal twang of many of the music's greatest practitioners. It was impossibly deep, a spare bass that made no attempt at prettification and seldom varied in timbre or pitch. In song it did not vary greatly from its conversational tone, and it rarely pleaded or cajoled or sought through any extraordinary means to convince its listener of the truth of what he or she was hearing. It did not swoop or soar or thrill its auditors with wide-ranging forays through the musical scales. It was not versatile or technically accomplished or beautiful in any conventional sense, and it was raised most often against a plain accompaniment of strummed acoustic guitar, electric guitar played as a rhythm instrument, bass, and drums, to an unvarying beat the singer characterized as "boom-chicka-boom." Incapable of histrionics, it was both stark and substantial, and absolutely convincing in its authenticity; it left little doubt that the singer knew of what he sang. It was dead honest, without adornment or ornamentation. Neither imitative nor imitated, it was absolutely distinctive, and an instrument of far greater virtuosity than it initially appeared: "a deep well of simple, profound American music," in the words of music journalist Bill Flanagan. "Any voice that can encompass and convey pride, humor, piety, rebellion, patriotism, larceny, solemnity, tragedy, rowdiness, heart-break, and love has great range."

"Well, you wonder why I always dress in black," the man onstage sang now. "Why you never see bright colors on my back / And why does my appearance seem to have a somber tone / Well, there's a reason for the things that I have on."

He was rich now, and happy, at peace with himself and his past, delivered of the demons that had almost destroyed him but never of some deep, ineradicable sadness born of the recollections of the cotton fields that his father and older brother had hacked from the swampy bottomland of the big river, where at age four he had begun to help his family earn their oh-so-precarious livelihood by carrying buckets of water to them as they worked. His songs had taken him far from those mean fields; he had sold millions of records, made millions of dollars, and attained a level of stardom and celebrity and respect that few country singers had ever known. Yet those fields still seemed very close, as did the strength of his yearning to escape them by any means possible. "Hard work?" he said once to an interviewer who asked him how his days in the fields had shaped his character. "Chopping cotton and picking cotton is drudgery. I don't know how much good it did me. I don't know how much good drudgery does anybody." And he remembered that there were many, poorer even than he had been and no less desperate or hardworking, who never escaped.

"I wear the black for the poor and beaten down / Living in the hopeless, hungry side of town / I wear it for the prisoner who has long paid for his crimes / But is there

because he's a victim of his times." The singer's prison concerts were legendary, his sympathy for and songs about those behind bars so well known that it was often incorrectly assumed that he had done hard time himself. Though he had been arrested several times in his hell-raising days, he had never spent more than a night or two in jail, yet he sang with an empathy born, if not of actual confinement, of knowledge of what it is like to be imprisoned by circumstance and of his long struggle with his own self-destructive impulses, which had led him to behavior society deemed criminal and had made him one of the first of country music's "outlaws." "I don't see anything good come out of a prison," he said often. "You put them in like animals and tear the soul and guts out of them, and let them out worse than they went in."

"I wear the black for those who've never read / Or listened to the words that Jesus said." Hymns and gospel music were the first songs the singer had known, and he had started his musical career hoping to make gospel records, only to be told that there was no market for them. With several secular hit singles under his belt, he

A housewife reads a magazine while listening to a broadcast from a battery-operated radio in the 1930s. To escape the drudgery of the day's cotton picking, young Johnny Cash huddled over his family's radio almost every night, entranced by the sounds of the musicians he heard on the "Grand Ole Opry," a country music program broadcast from Nashville, Tennessee.

17

had left his first record company for, among other things, the opportunity to make a gospel album, and he had long "tithed" a portion of his music to religious themes. But the despair of disbelief was familiar to this descendant of several generations of Baptist preachers. There had always been in him since his early years a kind of restlessness and sorrow, what his mother called "nervousness," and he had seen many things, first and foremost the painful death of a beloved brother, that made him question whether God really was merciful or just. In the feverish first excitement of stardom he had succumbed to the various temptations of the road and lost, he thought, his God forever. But his faith had returned to him, and with it balance, health, an acceptance of life's various mysteries, and the consoling belief that everything happens for a purpose.

"Well, we're doing mighty fine I do suppose / In our streak-of-lightning car and fancy clothes," sang the man who had been the youngest member ever inducted into the Country Music Hall of Fame. "But just so we're reminded of the ones who are held back / Up front there ought to be a man in black," sang the outlaw whose outrageous personal conduct had led to his being banned from the stage of the Grand Ole Opry, country music's foremost showcase, and who had risked his career challenging the nation's disc jockeys when they refused to play his songs of protest over America's shameful treatment of its Native American population.

"I wear it for the sick and lonely old / For the reckless ones whose bad trip left them cold," he sang. The singer had walked on the wild side: for nearly 10 years his addiction to amphetamines and tranquilizers had threatened to make of him the saddest kind of country music legend, the tormented, hell-raising singer who died too young, like his idols Jimmie Rodgers and Hank Williams, the latter dead at age 29 in the back of a limousine from "too much living." By the time he succeeded in getting straight, the dark myth of the Man in Black's personal excesses nearly overshadowed his accomplishments as one of America's foremost musical storytellers and chroniclers, and his name was associated as much with harrowing stories of late nights, gunplay, missed appearances, trashed hotel rooms, motor vehicle accidents, drug busts, and overdoses as it was with hit records. He was wrecked in mind and body, paranoid, delusional, malnourished; onstage he was, in the words of Bill Flanagan, often "frightening . . . emaciated . . . twitching, shaking, bug-eyed, and wired. He looked like the wildest punk rocker you ever saw."

"I wear the black in mourning for the lives that could have been / Each week we lose a hundred fine young men." The song had been written in 1971, at the height of the Vietnam War, when the nightly newscasts often led with the weekly body count of U.S. and Vietnamese dead and wounded and thousands of young Americans were protesting their country's involvement in the war, which had left the nation bitterly divided. The country music establishment, like most of its audience, tended to be extremely conservative and patriotic, the "silent majority" that President Richard M. Nixon would appeal to in the course of his successful campaign for reelection in 1972, but the Man in Black went his own way. "Don't ever tell anybody how John Cash feels about *anything* unless I've told you in the last few minutes," he had been known to snap at those who attempted to speak for him on political issues.

He had first escaped from the cotton fields many years before by enlisting in the armed services, like so many other young men from the rural South, and he was proud of his service in the air force, of his nation, and of its history. But whereas during the Vietnam War years many of his country music contemporaries, most notably Merle

The Man in Black's songs are often tales of the lovelorn and bereft, of coal miners and convicts, of forgotten heroes and hoboes, of the faithful and the fallen, of farmers and workingmen, and of the alone and forsaken.

Haggard, reached the top of the charts preaching a love-it-or-leave-it philosophy of flag-waving patriotism, undeviating support for the government, and outright scorn for the youth culture of the 1960s, the Man in Black took a more complex position. While Haggard was singing the praises of Muskogee, Oklahoma, a place where no one smoked marijuana or took "trips on LSD," "Old Glory" still waved at the courthouse, and "even squares [could] have a ball," the Man in Black urged his audience to "let the lonely voice of youth" tell them "what is truth"; befriended, recorded songs by, and wrote songs with Bob Dylan, the prophet of protest and voice of the counterculture; booked rock and roll acts on his television show; fought network censors and sponsors to allow folksinger Pete Seeger, who had long been blacklisted for his leftist political positions, to appear as his guest on the program; and recorded songs by Kris Kristofferson, a longhaired, shaggy-bearded singer and songwriter regarded with suspicion as a hippie doper renegade by the country music establishment. While Nixon campaigned successfully for presidential office as the self-proclaimed candidate of law and order, the Man in Black gave concerts in prison. Recognizing that most of the young men serving in Vietnam were either those who, because of their impoverished backgrounds, had no choice about serving or for whom the military represented, as it had for him, the sole opportunity for economic advancement or escape—indeed, 80 percent of the 2.5 million enlisted men who served in the U.S. armed forces in Vietnam came from poor or working-class backgrounds—he urged support for the troops and visited Vietnam to sing for them while expressing skepticism for the rightness of the American cause: "And I wear it for the thousands who have died / Believing that the Lord was on their side."

Though he has not lived everything he sings about, few singers seem to speak so deeply from experience as the

Man in Black. "Well there are things that never will be right, I know / And things need changing everywhere you go." His music, through almost four decades of performing, has never changed; bedrock simple, yet concerned with the deepest human mysteries, it transcends the narrow definition of country and wins admirers among each new generation to whom it is introduced. Bruce Springsteen, in inducting the Man in Black to the Rock and Roll Hall of Fame in 1991, cited the "extraordinary honesty" of his vocals and songs; Bob Dylan opined that if Johnny Cash were not in the Rock and Roll Hall of Fame, there was no sense in having one. (The Man in Black had been present at the creation, of course, with Elvis Presley, Jerry Lee Lewis, and Carl Perkins in the small storefront studio in Memphis where rock and roll had been born.) "In his voice there is a kind of wandering spirit," said Bono, lead singer of the Irish rock group U2, in explaining why he asked the Man in Black to record with the group for their 1993 smash album *Zooropa*. "He's cool . . . and dangerous."

"But till we start to make a move to make a few things right / You'll never see me wear a suit of white," the Man in Black sang, the deep, haunting voice driving the song urgently to its conclusion. Timeless and essential, his voice, presence, and songs—tales of the lovelorn and bereft, of coal miners and killers, of forgotten heroes and hoboes, of the faithful and the fallen, of farmers and workingmen, of the alone and the forsaken—have created a quintessentially American legend. "Pictures from life's other side," Hank Williams called his own songs in the same vein; "Winners got scars too," the Man in Black was fond of saying. He brought the song to a close, strumming hard on his Martin: "Oh, I'd love to wear a rainbow every day / And tell the world that everything is okay / But I'll try to carry off a little darkness on my back / Till things are brighter / I'm the man in black."

2 ★ Five Feet High and Rising

ACCORDING TO THE MOST FAMOUS member of the line, the first Cash came to North America in 1673. William Cash was a Scottish mariner who settled in Westmoreland County, Virginia, in that year. Among the more illustrious and prosperous families of the county, which lies between the Potomac and Rappahannock rivers, were the Washingtons, whose most famous scion, George, would be born there in 1732. By the time Washington was taking command of the Continental Army in defense of the 13 colonies' right to independence, the Cashes, no doubt in search of land and freedom from the heavy hand of the tax collector, had relocated westward to Amherst and Bedford counties, also in Virginia, in the shadows of the Alleghenies, where they were farmers and planters. Several served as soldiers for the American cause in the Revolution.

By the end of the first decade of the 19th century, Moses Cash, moved by that restless spirit that kept extending America's frontiers, had established a homestead in all-but-unsettled Henry County, Georgia. When in the closing months of the Civil War the homesteads and plantations of Georgia were

---

Cotton pickers labor in a field in Arkansas. Ray Cash, Johnny's father, was a hardworking cotton sharecropper, who as a farmer had been able to feed his increasingly large family—until the collapse of the cotton prices during the Great Depression.

23

ravaged by the vengeful Union troops of General William Tecumseh Sherman, Reuben Cash, who had fought for the Confederacy, loaded his family and remaining belongings in a couple of ox-drawn wagons and set out west across the Mississippi River, finally settling around 1866 near Rison, Arkansas, the county seat of Cleveland County, in the southern part of the state, where he farmed cotton. One of his sons, William Henry Cash—named after the first Cash in America and the beloved but abandoned Henry County in Georgia—married a woman named Rebecca, another Civil War refugee, from Virginia. Some of Rebecca's ancestors were apparently Native Americans, most likely Cherokee; according to some sources, her grandmother was a full-blooded Cherokee. In addition to farming, William Henry was a Baptist preacher, as were his father-in-law (another Confederate veteran of the Civil War) and two of his brothers-in-law.

Together, William Henry and Rebecca had 12 children, only 8 of whom survived infancy. The youngest, Ray Cash, was born on a cotton farm in Cleveland County, Arkansas, on May 13, 1897. Thirty-five years later, on February 26 in Kingsland, a once-prosperous farm center in the same county, the fourth of Ray's seven children would be born. Ray and his wife of 12 years, Carrie Rivers Cash, named the third of their four sons J. R., though the quiet, restless boy was called more commonly by his father by the affectionate nickname Shoo-doo. The boy began using the name John sometime later on, possibly when he joined the air force; "Johnny" was

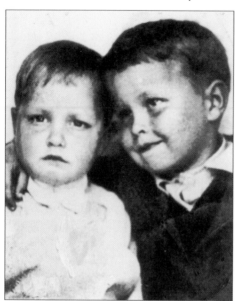

J. R. (left), nicknamed Shoo-doo by his father, and his brother Jack appear in a photograph from the early 1930s.

the creation of the legendary founder of Sun Records, Sam Phillips, for whom he recorded his first songs. Ray and Carrie's other six children, in order of birth, were Roy, Louise, Jack, Reba, Joann, and Tommy.

Like generations of Cashes before him, Ray was a small farmer who planted cotton for money on half the land he worked and food crops for his family on the remaining portion. With just an eighth-grade education, Ray had left his parents' spread in 1916, following the death of his mother, to enlist in the army. After duty in Deming, New Mexico, as a member of a patrol that was guarding the border against incursions by the Mexican bandit Pancho Villa, he was sent in the last days of World War I to France, where he guarded German prisoners of war and supply depots and managed to "lose" a supply train when he dallied too long with a mademoiselle in Saint-Lazare who was "learning me French." After three years in the service he returned to Cleveland County and took a job near Kingsland cutting down oak and cypress trees to make pilings for a bridge being built across the Saline River. During the course of this employment he stayed, at the cost of a dollar a day for meals and board, at the home of a family named Rivers. Carrie, one of the Rivers girls, often served the woodcutters their meals; she and Ray Cash were married on August 18, 1920. Roy, their first child, followed 13 months later.

By the time J. R. was born the United States was in the third year of an unprecedented nationwide economic collapse known as the Great Depression. Indeed, 1932 would prove to be one of the worst years of the crisis, which continued, with varying degrees of intensity, until the nation's entrance into World War II in December 1941. In 1932, the rate of unemployment in the United States reached 25 percent; the following year, 16 million Americans—one-third of the labor force—would find themselves without work.

The first segment of the American economy to feel the depression's effect, and the segment that would be hardest hit, was agriculture. For men like Ray Cash, farming had always been a precarious livelihood, dependent on the vagaries of nature and the vicissitudes of the marketplace. But with cotton fetching $125 for a 500-pound bale, as it did in 1928, and with the food crops grown on his spread, he had always been able to feed his increasingly large family, even if genuine prosperity somehow managed to elude him.

American farmers, however, worked too hard. Throughout the 1920s, agricultural production—particularly that of wheat and cotton—steadily rose, far outstripping the demand of the American marketplace for such products. In the previous decade these surpluses had been sold at profitable prices in Europe, where World War I had disrupted continental agricultural production. In the wake of the war, with the United States undertaking to provide food and economic relief to the war-torn nations of Europe, its own farmers were encouraged to expand production and increase the number of acres under tillage, most notably by borrowing money under newly liberal credit policies and by purchasing and using modern mechanized equipment.

The result was a much more productive and efficient American agricultural economy, but as American relief efforts in Europe took effect and the European economy began to recover, American farmers found themselves producing far more than the U.S. marketplace alone could absorb, with an ever-shrinking overseas marketplace as well. Agricultural production in the United States increased steadily throughout the 1920s, but farm income declined by almost half. While the American industrial economy was reaching new heights of prosperity, prices for farm products dropped constantly throughout the decade, with wheat, for example, selling for less than one-third of what it had 10 years earlier. The collapse in cotton prices was even more calamitous; by 1932 the 500-pound bale of cotton that Ray Cash had sold for $125 four years earlier was fetching just $25.

As such prices for agricultural products were actually below the lowest cost possible to produce them, farming had literally become a losing proposition. In these circumstances farmers found it difficult to keep up with their rent or mortgage payments or to pay off the debts incurred in borrowing to buy land, implements, seeds, and other provisions and necessities. Throughout the 1920s, as conditions worsened for farmers, the situation for their creditors grew desperate as well. Unable to collect on the debts owed them, landowners, many of whom rented out acreage; rural banks; manufacturers of plows, combines, tractors, and farming equipment; seed companies; railroad and freight concerns; operators of grain elevators and stockyards; and other industries vitally connected with agriculture found it increasingly difficult to meet their own obligations, and their economic situation suffered accordingly. The crisis fed off itself; credit was tightened, making it more difficult for all segments of the agricultural economy, from the farmer to the banker, to conduct business. Long before the nationwide banking crisis that heralded the collapse of the entire U.S. economy, rural banks were failing at an enormous rate. When the stock market crashed in late October 1929, ushering in the greatest economic catastrophe in American history, the consequences for the economy at large mirrored those that had already prevailed for many years in the agricultural segment.

Ray Cash had never had the opportunity to take advantage of the government's agricultural policies to expand his acreage or buy modern mechanized equipment. The land he tilled was not his own, and the plow he used to break the soil was hitched to the back of a mule, not a tractor. Overproduction had never been a problem for Ray Cash and others like him; a successful year meant all the debts paid off at the end of the harvest and enough food on the table so that no one went hungry. Even so, sharecroppers—in 1930, 63 percent of Arkansas's farmers worked land they did not own—were still the first to feel the effects of the depression when it set in.

For much of the 1920s Ray had worked a spread on a large farm owned by his brother Dave near Kingsland, but by the end of the decade it had grown increasingly difficult to make ends meet. The Cotton Belt railroad ran through the Cash place, and by the winter of 1929 the family had grown accustomed to the sight of people— men, mostly, but sometimes women and children, too— hitching a ride on the rails to anywhere they might find work or a place to stay. Some days all the boxcars were filled, and the transients rode on the roofs or the "blinds" (between cars). By the early 1930s almost half the population of Cleveland County was on government relief, most of the needy being farm families.

Ray Cash was known in his community as a high-strung but extremely hardworking man. When farming went bust he took whatever work was available, most often cutting wood or sometimes working at a sawmill or laying track and doing odd jobs on the railroad. For 15 cents an hour he would cut down hickory, pine, and gum trees, which would then be hauled by mule to the sawmill across the county line in Fordyce. Most such work required that he walk several miles to and from the site, but at least, unlike so many other men, he did not have to leave his family behind while he looked for employment.

As the depression deepened, wages declined even further, and Ray Cash was lucky to bring home 25 or 50 cents per day when he could find work; sometimes he was paid in wood or food. The family moved several times, to Fordyce and Saline, where they lived in a house without windows, and then back to Kingsland. Now, more often than ever before, the desperate men who showed up at their door asking to earn a couple of cents by splitting wood had to be turned away without work or food. Ray put food on his family's table by hunting; a box of shells for his .22 cost 20 cents, and he could not afford to miss any of the rabbits, possums, raccoons, and squirrels he shot at.

Sometimes his skill with a rifle earned him cash: when the government decided to drive up the price of beef by paying subsidies to ranchers and farmers to thin their herds, Ray's brother hired him to put down 50 of his worst animals. Working at point-blank range, he needed just 50 shots to finish the job, but the bloody work and the sight of his brother's hogs rooting voraciously among the carcasses afterward left him with nightmares that lasted for weeks. "I could see those scrawny cows with their heads hanging down and their eyes just looking at me. I wasn't very proud of it," he said. The job paid "a couple of dollars."

Proud of never being forced to hobo around, Ray Cash left his family just once, when a man offered him and a number of Cleveland County men a job at the good wage of 35 cents per hour, dismantling a chemical plant in Charleston, Mississippi, 150 miles to the east. With a friend, he hopped a freight and rode the blinds to Memphis and then Charleston, managing to stay one step ahead of the railroad detectives and nearly freezing to death en route. He arrived to find the locals up in arms about the influx of outside labor and offering to perform the work at a lower wage; though his employer remained loyal to those he had originally hired, the Arkansas men learned to travel in groups for fear of being waylaid and beaten up by the Mississippians. The job lasted 21 straight days, and Ray was able to send $60 ahead to his family while he rode the freights back home.

The money and a package of clothes he had also mailed arrived long before him, leading his family to assume that he had been killed somewhere along the way. During the depression, many men never came back from such journeys, and on his return home, in Brinkley, Arkansas, Ray Cash did in fact have a close encounter with a notorious railyard bull (policeman), who yanked him and his friend off their train. "That was the only time I ever stood and let a man talk to me like that," Ray Cash, poor but proud, later said about the incident. Not long afterward the bull made the mistake of doing the same thing to another hobo, who pulled out a gun and shot him dead.

With the accession of Franklin D. Roosevelt to the presidency in 1933, the outlook for most Americans improved. Although full economic recovery was still far off, Roosevelt immediately inspired confidence in his own and the nation's ability to cope with the crisis. "The only thing we have to fear is fear itself," he said in his inaugural address, and he quickly set about designing and implementing a number of revolutionary programs designed to provide relief, put people back to work, promote recovery, and significantly reform many aspects of American society and the economy.

As much as the actual content of these programs, it was Roosevelt's commitment to active government intervention in the crisis that restored the faith of most Americans. For the nation collectively, the depression was as profound a psychological or spiritual crisis as it was an economic one. It destroyed the

Families in the drought-stricken town of Tyronza, Arkansas, line up for food at a Red Cross aid station in 1931. Not only did the nation's farmers have to deal with the collapsed U.S. economy that made farming a losing proposition during the 1930s, but also with devastating droughts, dust storms, floods, and disease.

myth of limitless prosperity that had held sway for most Americans during the 1920s as well as the confidence of millions of Americans in themselves, in their ability to provide for their families, and in their government. For the countless people whom the depression had left unemployed and homeless, the insistence of Herbert Hoover, Roosevelt's predecessor, on laissez-faire economic policies, voluntarism, and individual initiative rather than broad-based government action as a solution for the nation's woes seemed like abandonment, less philosophical integrity than callous indifference, and in the last days of his administration a sense of overwhelming despair seemed to overtake the nation. "What was dead," wrote one observer, "was hope," and it was this quality that Roosevelt sought immediately to restore.

Roosevelt therefore took office pledging "action, and action now." For Ray Cash the most consequential of the many programs implemented by the new president in his famous first 100 days in office was the Federal Emergency Relief Administration (FERA), created for the express purpose of directly alleviating, in the form of relief payments, the hardship suffered by the estimated 30 million Americans who had been left without any source of income as a result of the Great Depression. For Hoover and those who shared his governmental philosophy, such payments represented an unacceptable intrusion—disturbingly akin to socialism—of the federal government into the private sector of the economy. Such disruptions as the Great Depression were an unfortunate but inevitable cyclical by-product of the American free-market economy, such traditional thinking held; given time and relative freedom from interference, the market would right itself.

But for Roosevelt the unprecedented scope and severity of the suffering created by the Great Depression called for similarly unprecedented responses on the part of the federal government. FERA was one such response. Its immediate and simple goal was to put money in the pockets of the country's neediest people and relieve human misery, restore the public's confidence, and enable such individuals, particularly in the rural sector of the economy, to again take their place as consumers. In time, as recovery began, FERA and other like-minded programs of the New Deal, as Roosevelt termed his domestic policy, would become even more ambitious in scope by seeking to reintegrate those ruined by the depression into the economy as productive individuals. Providing those rural poor who had been driven off the land with financial relief was a worthy goal, but without a corresponding program to reestablish them on their own land as producers and consumers in the agricultural economy, they in all likelihood would become dependent on a federal dole for their continued survival.

It was one of the most ambitious and innovative of the FERA programs that constituted a new deal for Ray Cash and his family. At 46 different sites across the nation's farm belt, the federal government bought land and redistributed it, in the form of resettlement colonies, to those deserving farmers who had been ruined by the depression. The program was not a giveaway; each participant would be expected to work for his land, and government administrators attempted to determine those with the best chance of success by carefully interviewing each candidate. Ray Cash explained the simple essence of the program: "We heard that we could buy 20 acres of land without any money down, and a house and a barn, and they would give us a mule, a cow and furnish groceries through the year until we had a crop and could pay it back, and we didn't have to pay until the crops came in."

With the price of cotton having climbed back to $50 a bale, Ray Cash returned to farming in 1933, but as a sharecropper, with no real prospect of possessing his own land. He therefore regarded the FERA program as a godsend, and in late 1934, dressed in his overalls—"They were about all he owned," said his oldest son, Roy—he traveled to the courthouse in Rison to apply for the program. "I told them I wanted to make a home for my family and myself," he said, but he returned to Kingsland somewhat discouraged by the six-page application form he had been asked to fill out, by the tenacity of the interviewer, and by the fact that there had been 20 men already in line when he arrived at the courthouse. There was room in the Arkansas program for just 500 families, and some had already been chosen; very probably only a handful would be selected from Cleveland County, because in all the 75 counties of Arkansas there was a total of nearly 40,000 farm families still on relief, and interviewers around the state had been deluged with applicants.

But Ray Cash, as the goverment men would soon discover as they began running their checks on his credentials, enjoyed an excellent reputation for hard work and upstanding character, and he was one of five Cleveland County men selected to settle what was originally titled Colonization Project Number One and would soon be known as the Dyess Colony, after the administrator of FERA in Arkansas, W. R. Dyess. On March 23, 1935, a pickup truck arrived in Kingsland to transport the Cashes, who had been given 24 hours' notice, and their meager belongings to Dyess.

The Dyess Colony was 16,000 acres of flat, black Mississippi Delta land in Mississippi County, Arkansas, which is tucked into the northeast corner of the state between the St. Francis and Mississippi rivers, just below the southernmost extension of the state of Missouri and across the big river from Tennessee. The land would prove to be fertile, with thick, rich topsoil—deposited over the ages by the Mississippi on its periodic unruly wanderings over its banks—hundreds of feet deep, but it was uncleared and swampy, a wilderness more hospitable at that point to rattlesnakes and water moccasins than to farmers. Since May 1934, a crew of 2,000 men, taken from Arkansas's relief rolls, had been at work, at the rate of $5 per day, transforming this wasteland into the Dyess Colony. A railroad spur was laid down, its ties constructed from the same oak trees that were felled by the logging crews to establish a path for the railway. In the colony center itself, a cooperative general store and a small café were thrown up. Sixteen gravel roads spoked out from the hub of the colony to the 502 20-acre homesteads that surrounded it, where 10-man construction crews threw up plain five-room farmhouses in 16 hours. Each spread also featured a chicken coop, barn, and outhouse; there was no electricity or running water. Ninety miles of ditches were dug to drain the land. Anything beyond was up to the colonists themselves.

Johnny Cash's earliest memory is of his family's 27-hour, 250-mile trip through an icy, portentous rain from Kingsland to Dyess. He remembers the bitter cold as the family hunched together, trying to snatch a few hours' sleep before dawn with the truck pulled over outside Marion, Arkansas, and the lonesome feeling the sight of the silvery, icicle-laden trees alongside the muddy, rutted road gave him as he peered out the back of the truck.

The Cash place was Number 266, about two and one-half miles north of the colony center on Road Three. The freezing gray rain was still falling as the Cashes first laid eyes on their new home. "It was a nicer house than any we had lived in," Ray Cash remembered years later, freshly painted white with green trim, the paint buckets still on the floor inside. There were two big bedrooms, a kitchen, a dining room, a living room, and a front and back porch. The yard was underwater, though, as was most of their land, and tangled with underbrush; "That black mud," said Carrie Cash, who waded to the house carrying baby Reba in her arms, "stuck to your feet like glue." Nonetheless Ray, wearing a pair of hip waders, set out immediately to walk his property. What was not flooded was choked with trees and brush; at one point Ray fell into a stump hole and plunged into chest-deep icy water. He returned home shortly before dark, as the family was preparing to go to sleep on the wood floor of the living room. "We have some fine land," he announced.

The Cash farm in Dyess looked similar to this site—the yard was underwater and tangled with brush and trees.

Technically, that soaked acreage was not yet Ray's. He was what the program termed a licensee, meaning that he would not be given a deed and mortgage to the property until he demonstrated his ability to clear it and convert it to productive cotton fields. The colony center office advanced him the carefully calculated sum of $253.59 in the form of "doodlum," as the colony scrip was known, which was to be redeemed for food, tools, and supplies to tide the family over until they got their first crop in. The advance was added to the cost of their home and land and the charges for the move, all of which the Cashes would be expected to pay back out of the money earned from their cotton crop.

Even though he did not yet legally possess his land, Ray Cash felt an immediate pride in his homestead, for this new deal for the family was far better than any hand it had been dealt before: "It gave our entire family a new start. We'd always been sharecropping on other people's land. We felt more free. . . . It was the first land we owned, and we felt ourselves equal with anybody."

The work required of Ray Cash to redeem the government's offer to him was endless and backbreaking. When the water receded, Ray and his oldest son, Roy, who was

35

not yet 14, set out to clear the property. Using double-bit axes and a two-man crosscut saw, they worked from the highest ground downward, dynamiting or burning out stumps as they went. Each kept a hoe nearby as protection against equally deadly water moccasins and rattlers. Their day lasted from sunrise until past sunset; they usually finished up by the light of a kerosene lamp.

"It was about as rough going as a feller'd want," a neighbor, "Goat" Rogers, remembered of those early days in the colony. Though it was late in the year to start putting in a crop, the Cashes, with the help of Joe, their trusty mule, managed to clear, plow, and plant three acres—two in cotton and one in corn, beans, tomatoes, strawberries, and sweet potatoes. The family's cotton crop yielded three bales, which sold for $50 each at the colony center, allowing the Cashes to make the first payment on their land. The grain and vegetables were used to feed themselves and their animals—Joe, a milk cow, and some pigs and chickens. The next summer, young J. R. first started helping out in the fields by hauling water in buckets to his parents and older siblings as they chopped away the weeds that threatened to choke the cotton plants.

Colonists prepare corn for canning at the Dyess community cannery in the 1930s. The colony was run as a cooperative—the colonists depended on one another for their own prosperity.

"We were never hungry," Roy Cash remembered. "There might be beans twice a day and bread and gravy for breakfast, but there was always plenty." For Ray Cash the ultimate payoff was worth almost any hardship: "We made up our minds to make a home of it when we moved there. Times were pretty rough, but we didn't get disheartened." All the homesteaders at Dyess came from similar situations—"so many of our neighbors were in the same category as we were," Ray Cash remembered, "not destitute, because we were never destitute, but needy"—and a communal spirit prevailed. "Lots of times," said Ray, "we'd all work together clearing land. We'd cut down trees and have 'log rollings'—pile up the logs and burn them. The women would get together for projects like quilting or stuffing mattresses with ginned cotton." The Cashes, remembered always by their neighbors in later years as "good Christian people," enjoyed a special reputation for generosity toward others. "They was accommodating. Nice neighbors," said their friend Frank Huff. "They'd help you in any way they could. Old man Cash—he was kinda high-strung, but he was a hustler. He was a worker." When the Cashes finished picking their first cotton crop that December, Ray went to work building houses and barns on the last few unoccupied homesteads. The colonists had to depend on one another, for their own prosperity was dependent on that of their neighbors. Dyess was run as a cooperative—"I grew up under socialism," Johnny Cash likes to say—meaning that its residents' crops were sold cooperatively, so as to obtain a better price than they would if sold individually.

Ray remained handy with a rifle as well. By 1936 much of the Cash land was still little more than "jungle," as Johnny would later describe it, and some untamed inhabitant of that wilderness developed the habit of stealing hens at night from the family's chicken coop. So Ray staked out the henhouse and killed the culprit—a huge 27-pound wildcat—with his shotgun. Colonists came from miles around to see the magnificent pelt he took from the animal, which was so large that J. R., Jack, and Reba could all stretch out on it at one time. Ray was proud of his trophy, but his wife thought it could be put to more practical use. Carrie Cash loved to read, so one day while Ray was in the fields she traded the wildcat pelt with a salesman for a subscription to the *Kansas City Star* newspaper. Her husband, she later recalled, "didn't like it much," but the isolation of such rural homesteads could be overwhelming, and a newspaper represented a much needed link with the outside world.

Near the end of 1936 the Cashes invested in the most common instrument used by farm families to keep in touch with the bigger world outside their acreage—a battery-operated upright radio, ordered from another indispensable means of outside contact, the *Sears, Roebuck Catalogue.* By that point they felt secure enough to indulge in a little luxury, for they had more of their property under plow, the land was fertile, and the colony itself seemed to be solidly established. With its large farm families, Dyess had a population of about 3,000, and the colony center now featured a service station, garage, harness shop, grain mill, blacksmith shop, printing shop, cannery, icehouse, sorghum mill, cotton gin, library, school, and 20-bed hospital. A monthly and then weekly newspaper, the *Colony Herald,* reported on local events. A Cub Scout troop and a 4-H club had been formed, and a two-day fair was held in September. First Lady Eleanor Roosevelt visited Dyess to congratulate the colonists on their hard work, as did Harry Hopkins, who headed the New Deal's relief programs.

The colonists seemed to have every reason to believe, as they were told by Colonel Lawrence Westbrook, who oversaw such resettlement programs for Hopkins, that they had escaped the darkest uncertainties of the depression.

A resettled family poses in front of their Dyess home in the early 1930s. By the end of 1936, the Cash family had more of their property under plow and could afford the luxury of a battery-operated radio, an essential link to the outside world.

"You may have to draw in your belt and do without some things that you need," Westbrook told the residents of Dyess, "but never again need you be assailed by the terrible fear that you and your family will have no roof over your heads, nor that stark hunger will overcome you."

And then, just after the New Year, 1937, as Johnny Cash would chronicle in one of his early hits, it started to rain. Each day the icy rain came down, until the mighty Mississippi, barely held 15 miles away to the east by levees and barricades of sandbags, was 15 feet above flood level. Each day at the Cash place the family watched as the water rose to the level of another step on the porch. How high is the water? the children asked their parents each day; Frank Huff had made it to the colony center, where according to his measuring stick, it was three feet high "and rising." Out at the Cash place it was higher; when it reached five feet high and rising, as Johnny Cash would later sing, Ray sent his family to higher ground.

The front page of the June 12, 1936, issue of the *Colony Herald* features a photograph of First Lady Eleanor Roosevelt's visit to Dyess Colony.

★★★★★ Guess Things
3 ★ Happen
★★★★★ That Way

I T HAD RAINED for almost two weeks without letup when Ray Cash ordered his wife and four youngest children to leave their home. On January 18, 1937, a homemade boat carried them and their portable possessions to a bus, which was taking the outlying families of the colony to the safer haven of Wilson, 12 miles away. Colonists who lived closer to the colony center were transported to Wilson in railroad boxcars. Both the railway and the road were under water, but the bus ran the greater risk of accident; the way to Wilson had been staked out with tall flag-bearing posts so that the vehicle would not careen off the highway, and from the windows the passengers could see bridges that had been torn away by the rampaging river floating on the floodwaters. (Many of the roads into and out of Dyess, as elsewhere in the rural South, were built on embankments that placed them above the surrounding fields.) From Wilson, many of the displaced went on by train to a refugee camp in Little Rock, the state

Automobiles navigate a sandbagged highway during the Mississippi flood of 1937. Almost a week after sending his wife and four youngest children to safety in Kingsland, Ray and his oldest son had to abandon their attempt to stave off the big river when it inundated their property.

capital, where they were housed in army tents, but Carrie Cash took her family by rail back to her people in Kingsland.

For the almost-five-year-old Johnny, the experience was something of a great adventure, as he told his biographer, Christopher S. Wren, author of *Winners Got Scars Too: The Life and Legends of Johnny Cash*: "It was late at night, and everyone on the train was sleeping. My mother, I remember, had dressed me in my new suit. [The suit was a Tom Sawyer special, purchased for $1.25 in the Dyess cooperative, and constituted all of Johnny's "good" clothing; otherwise he wore jeans or overalls.] I kept running up and down the aisle. Down near Stuttgart, Arkansas, we weren't moving over five miles an hour, because the water was clear over the tracks. They were afraid they might hit a big log over the tracks if they went any faster. I remember a lot of the women and children were crying because they were so afraid and upset."

After six more days Ray and Roy Cash were forced to end their efforts to prevent the big river from reclaiming the land they had hacked from the Arkansas swamps. They propped open the front doors of the house so that if the waters rolled in, they would roll right back out again without leaving a huge deposit of silt inside. The chickens were taken from the coop and left on the living room floor, as was the family's rabbit hound, with the butchered pieces of a 50-pound ham. The corncrib was left open in the barn so the pigs could eat, and Joe the mule and the milk cow were led through the rising waters to the communal pen in the colony center. On January 24, with a prayer and much regret, Ray Cash and his oldest son abandoned their New Deal homestead to the flood. Only one farmer in the entire colony remained on his spread. As Ray and Roy left Dyess for Wilson and thence to Kingsland, armed lawmen, sent by the state, were beginning to patrol the colony in boats to guard against looters.

Against all odds, the levees and sandbags held, and the wind, which had been driving the waters from out of the east, shifted and then abated. The rain stopped, and the floodwaters slowly receded. On February 16 the Cashes returned to their land, where they discovered that they had been much more fortunate than many of their neighbors. Their house had been left dirty and wet, but they had not lost anything of significance; their animals had survived and even multiplied—the chickens had laid eggs on the couch, and the sow had given birth to five piglets—and the outbuildings were all intact, though Ray Cash had to kill twentysome poisonous snakes that had found safety in the rafters of his barn.

Many others had not been so fortunate. A significant number of the little two-bedroom houses had been rendered uninhabitable, filled with mud and silt, and livestock was scattered around the countryside. Many animals fell prey to the packs of voracious feral dogs that now roamed the colony as famished refugees from their former homes. Many families had nothing to eat; many of the homesteaders came down with pneumonia from the pervasive damp and cold, and died. Federal relief had to be organized for the aid of the colony.

But if the Lord taketh away, he also giveth, as all the Cashes knew so well from the Scripture and from their attendance at the First Baptist Church on Sunday mornings, Sunday nights, and Wednesday evenings. The silt the floodwaters had dumped on the Cash land only made it that much richer, and in March, Ray and the family were able to get eight acres of cotton planted. The year-end harvest was the richest the family would ever know, as those eight acres each yielded two bales.

By 1938 all of Ray's 20 acres had been cleared for planting—he would eventually grow 18 different crops

The Dyess library was housed in the community building, located at the colony's center. Rebuilding after the devastating flood, the colony expanded its center to include a movie theater, post office, and drugstore.

on his spread—and on February 5 of that year he was rewarded for his industry with a deed to his land. With his deed came a share in the Dyess Colony cooperative. That same year Ray Cash made his first deposit—$25—in the colony bank and felt he had "really done something." There was even enough left over for Carrie Cash to purchase, for $37, a used upright piano. The colony, too, recovered quickly from the flood. By 1938 there were 637 homesteads, and the colony center had expanded to include a movie theater, a drugstore, and a post office.

Life in the Dyess colony proceeded according to the seasonal ritual of agriculture. Late winter—February or early March—was time for Ray Cash to hitch up the mule to the wagon for the trip into the colony center, where he negotiated the loan for that season's crops with "that cigarette-smoking, Coke-sucking woman at the administration building," as Johnny later described her. Back on his farm, he got behind the mule again and plowed the land. April was planting time; the long hot summer, with endless days of temperatures approaching 100 degrees Fahrenheit, was spent chopping away with a hoe at the weeds that sprang up around the cotton plants and threatened to choke them. Everyone in the family old enough to walk on their own chopped cotton. Each of the children had additional chores as well, to be performed early in the mornings, before classes when school was in session. J. R. was responsible for feeding the chickens and chopping wood for the stove; the children, like their parents, rose with the sun. After school, it was back to the fields to chop cotton.

The only real break in the routine came on Sundays, when the family attended church services, which occupied most of the day. Some Saturdays one or another of the children might ride with their father into Dyess proper to pick up supplies. For young J. R., such trips were a rare treat. "I remember riding to town on our two-wheeler cart," he said years later. "We had a shopping list—flour, tobacco, sugar, salt, coal oil, matches. We used doodlum, and with it I could get a nickel's worth of candy. The counter was on the right, and the sugar and stick candy were in big glass jars, but the man that ran the store would always give us more than a nickel's worth. They had a clothing section in the store. I had one good Tom Sawyer suit, but I usually wore denim jeans. I'd walk through the section looking at all the clothes. When you know you can't have things, you don't want for them. I always got something to eat when I was hungry, and the rest didn't bother me."

Picking started in August and lasted until December, with everyone in the family again expected to do their share. Ray, Carrie, and the older children each hauled a nine-foot sack that would hold 75 pounds of cotton into the fields; the littler children used smaller sacks sewn especially for them by their mother. Ray was the family's champion picker; "on the fifteenth day of September 1931," he remembered ever thereafter, he picked 453 pounds of cotton, a personal record. As a teenager, Johnny says, he regularly picked 350 pounds a day, though his father remembers 250 pounds being more typical. Among the children, the best picker was Johnny's older sister, Louise, who could often match her father. For all the hard work that it involved, "pickin' time" was also, as Johnny Cash would write in his hit song of the same name, eagerly anticipated, for it was the one time of the year the family would actually have any money. All transactions the rest of the year were done on credit or with doodlum, with the accounts settled once the crops were in. If it had been a good year, there might be some money left over after Ray had settled up with everyone.

The winter months, once the crops were in, were time for other chores. Ray Cash spent approximately half the days of each month working for the Works Progress Administration (WPA), a New Deal job-creation program. Most of this work consisted of public improvement projects, such as clearing drainage ditches, resurfacing roadways, or building bridges, at a wage of 40 cents an hour. "Those Cashes were hard workers," Frank Huff remembered. "We could work on the WPA twelve days a month, then Ray'd go and work on his own place, too." Back home, the first frost was invariably followed by Ray's pronouncement that "it's hog-killing time," and he

In 1939 men work on the Arkansas River Flood Control Project for the Works Projects Administration, a New Deal job-creation program. By 1943 when the WPA ended its activities, it had provided work for more than 8 million unemployed.

46

would head for the pens with his .22. With no electricity or refrigeration, freezing weather was a necessity to salt and preserve meat. Besides pork, the family lived in the winter months on what they had grown earlier. "We grew everything the land would produce that we could eat. I canned enough in summer to keep us through the winter," Carrie Cash said. "When the vegetables got low, we made soup out of what was left. We didn't waste anything." And soon it would be time again for Ray Cash to hitch up the mule to the wagon and pay a visit to that cigarette-smoking, Coke-sucking woman down in the colony center.

It was a hard life, a lonely and isolated life in many ways, and if J. R. Cash did not complain about it, that did not necessarily mean that he did not have ideas of his own about living a different way when he got older. "John was probably the only one of us kids who worked on the farm and didn't complain," his sister Reba said, but that in itself was not an indication that he was content, for he rarely gave outward signs of what was going on inside. "He was the quietest one of the children," his mother remembers. "He hardly ever said anything. But he listened. He was drinking it all in." Family and friends invariably used the same words to describe him: quiet, restless, nervous, thoughtful, and shy. Though he saw an immense value and dignity in the way his family lived and took a pride nearly as great as his father's in their owning their own land, he decided early on that farming was not for him. "When we grew up," he said many years later, "it was second nature that we wouldn't live in Dyess when we were grown. It was the aim of every person to get a better job. But if I hadn't grown up there, I wouldn't be what I am now. It was the foundation for what I became."

Off the farm there were few diversions for a growing boy, few possibilities for a different kind of life. There was school, of course, but though obviously intelligent, J. R. Cash was mostly an indifferent student. Without trying, he could do more in class than much better prepared and more interested pupils, one of his teachers once told his mother, but he still mostly earned Cs and Ds, with better marks occasionally in those subjects that most interested him—English and history. "He'd make good grades when he'd try," his mother said, "but he didn't care about homework. He didn't do much of it." There were sports, but J. R.'s responsibilities at home kept him from playing on any of the Dyess school teams. He was a powerful swimmer, the best of the boys who congregated in their cutoffs at the Blue Hole, a popular bathing spot on one of the drainage ditches, and he fished for the region's outsized catfish and perch on the Tyronza River; one summer he even swam across the Mississippi below Memphis, and at age 18 he won an Arkansas State boys' swimming championship. But there was no way to swim out of Dyess.

For white rural southerners there were two time-honored means of relief from their life of eternal, repetitive toil: religion and music. (The same was largely true, in different ways, for black rural southerners as well, but because the world that Johnny Cash knew as a boy was virtually all white—the one less than socially progressive aspect of the Dyess Colony being that no blacks were accepted as homesteaders—it was the religion and music of white southerners that directly exerted the greatest influence on him.)

Agricultural societies tend to be extremely religious, attributing the hand of the divine to the otherwise inexplicable occurrences of the natural world that their livelihood, sustenance, and survival depend on, and the world of the white rural southerner was no exception. In the South that religion was invariably Protestant, largely Methodist, Baptist, or the various Pentecostal sects. The tenor of all three tended to be fatalistic, emphasizing humankind's sinful nature, the hardness of life in this world, and the joys of the salvation that the righteous would know in the hereafter, and stressing the literal truth of the words of the Bible.

As such, these faiths seemed only to emphasize verities about existence that the day-to-day life of rural southerners confirmed; rare was the poor farmer who had no firsthand experience of such biblical calamities as flood, pestilence, famine, drought, and fire. The scores of rivers that watered the South, making it so rich a region for agriculture and related endeavors, were also often the scourge of its inhabitants, overflowing their banks and wiping out in an instant what it had taken a lifetime to lay by.

The mortality rate among rural southerners, who well into the 20th century were often too impoverished and isolated to receive modern medical care, was far higher than the national average, particularly among the young. Diseases such as hookworm, diphtheria, whooping cough, pellagra, malaria, rickets, polio, scarlet fever, tuberculosis, and influenza—some of them directly related to the poverty and overall conditions of life in rural America—exacted an even more deadly toll in the South than elsewhere, and the Cashes were a most unusual family in not having lost a child in infancy.

The dreaded boll weevil constituted a veritable plague on cotton farmers throughout most of the South, if, fortuitously, not in Dyess; boll weevils and other insects, such as army worms and aphids, could leave a field stripped bare in just a few days.

Though few people starved to death, hunger was commonplace throughout the South, as were diseases associated with nutritional deficiencies such as pellagra and rickets, and throughout the 1930s hundreds of thousands of Americans were forced to go on the road in an

On Black Sunday, April 14, 1935, a blizzard of dust transforms daylight into night in western Kansas. The dust storms for many in the Dust Bowl became so unyielding that inhabitants warned of the wrath of God and "the end of the world."

attempt to keep food on the table: Johnny Cash retains vivid memories of the migrant workers who tramped into Dyess each picking season looking for a few days' work on which to feed their families.

In that same decade drought and gales combined to blow away the long-overworked soil of the Great Plains, converting 756 counties in 19 midwestern states—most notably Oklahoma, Kansas, Nebraska, Texas, and the Dakotas—into the so-called Dust Bowl. The winds blew for weeks on end, and the huge dust clouds covered the sky and blocked out the sun, transforming day into night and night into something as dark as the tomb. The "rolling black smoke" of the storms, as one observer described it, was visible as far east as Albany, New York, while in the heart of the Dust Bowl men literally vomited dirt; a variety of respiratory ailments related to the dust storms, known collectively as the "dust pneumonia," became commonplace. The sand covered fields, barns, homes, fences, and trees; the dust, according to one Oklahoma resident, "blew into the eyes, underneath the collar; undressing, there were specks of dust inside the buttonholes; in the morning it had gathered like fine snow along the window ledge; it penetrated even more, into the wiring of the house; and along the edges of the door . . . there was a rusty brown stain." At the height of the storms streetlights in Oklahoma were kept burning night and day for weeks on end. Residents of many Dust Bowl communities were certain that the storms represented the end of the world, a "doom" or "judgment" upon them by God, according to the depression-era balladeer Woody Guthrie.

Indeed, there was something about the very character of rural life, with its daily intimacy even in relatively prosperous times with the mysteries of life and death, that seemed to lend itself to a literal interpretation of Scripture. In his 1975 autobiography, *The Man in Black,* Johnny Cash recalls walking home at night along the raised gravel roads of the colony and, seeing the sky lit red along the horizon with the glow from forest or grass fires, which were frequent in the region, believing that he was actually looking at the fires of hell. "I remember being scared," he wrote. "Or I remember getting wakened in the middle of the night and looking out the window to see the glow from a grass fire and really shivering with fright that it might be hell."

On the farm, even before the trauma of the Great Depression, where death was always near, and displacement, in itself a kind of death for people raised on the land, and hunger just a bad crop or some calamity away, it did not seem so far-fetched that hell might be just over the horizon. Heaven might be farther off, but that, too, was in keeping with rural theology, wherein man's essentially wayward nature made it easier for him to sin than to be saved.

The congregation of a Pentecostal church in Memphis, Tennessee, poses for a group photograph in the early 1940s. J. R. Cash was initially frightened by the spiritual ecstasy he witnessed at Pentecostal services in Dyess but was delighted by the uninhibited music he heard played and sung there.

In the 1930s, for many thousands of Johnny Cash's fellow Arkies, and even more Okies from Arkansas's neighbor state to the west, the promised land was California, as articulated most famously in Guthrie's Dust Bowl ballads and by the indomitable Ma Joad, matriarch of the Okie clan whose travails are the subject of John Steinbeck's classic 1939 novel, *The Grapes of Wrath*. California is a "garden of Eden, a paradise for you and me" and a place where "the water tastes like wine," Guthrie sang. "I like to think how nice it's gonna be, maybe, in California," Ma Joad says. "Never cold. An' fruit ever'place, and people just bein' in the nicest places, little white houses in among the orange trees."

The Methodists, the Baptists, and the Pentecostals were all represented in Dyess, and young J. R. Cash had experience with the religious services of each. Ray Cash had been raised a Baptist, and Carrie Rivers Cash a Methodist. Although the couple and their children considered themselves members of the First Baptist Church, doctrinal differences mattered little to them, and they were also not-infrequent guests at the Methodist house of worship in Dyess as well as occasional participants in the raucous Pentecostal services at the Road Fifteen Church of God and the Church of God out on Road One. The initial impression J. R. took from his exposure to the religion of his forebears was fright, particularly at the Pentecostal services his mother loved to attend, where, overcome by the Holy Ghost, the participants would shout, speak in tongues, weep, moan, and writhe on the floor in spiritual ecstasy. But at the age of 12, during a two-week revival at the First Baptist Church he made, by walking to the altar and giving the preacher his hand, a "public show of repentance and acceptance of Jesus as Lord and Savior." That declaration was a "milestone" in his life, Cash later wrote, "the surrender of a young boy who had reached spiritual and moral accountability." By that time his beloved brother Jack, who was two years older, had already announced that he had been "called" to be a preacher.

There was one aspect of religious services that delighted J. R. Cash more than any other. If the preachers often terrified him with their sermons about man's wickedness and the pain of hellfire, the songs he heard in church exhilarated him. "I could see no joy in what they were doing," he admitted feeling, initially, about what he saw in his fellow congregants at the Pentecostal services, but from the beginning he felt different about the songs that were sung in church. "Those songs carried me away," he later wrote, "and they gave me a taste of heavenly things." The songs were best at the Church of God, where the music was often as uninhibited as the services. The Pentecostals allowed any kind of musical instrument at their services—guitars, mandolins, banjos, fiddles, tambourines, and even horns sometimes—and their songs used virtually every available folk music style, including jazz and ragtime.

Hymns and gospel songs were but one aspect of the incredibly rich musical culture of the American South. Modern country music is the commercial manifestation, many decades, many permutations, and innumerable influences later, of the folk music of the white rural South. That music had its roots in the ballads, hymns, reels, jigs, and other songs and instrumental pieces brought across the Atlantic with them by the first white settlers of the region, who were predominantly the peoples of the British Isles—the English, Welsh, Scottish, Irish, and Scotch-Irish. As these settlers moved inland from the coast, they carried their music with them. From the colonial days onward, music occupied a central place in southern culture, particularly in the life of the lower classes.

In America the music changed considerably, of course, though it retained much of its essential form, especially in the South—"the fertile crescent of country music," as two prominent musicologists have called it. The geographic isolation and agricultural way of life of most of the South's inhabitants, combined with a comparative lack of industrialization and urbanization and the homogeneous makeup of its population, encouraged the transmission and preservation of folk culture. New songs were made up, sometimes using old melodies, to reflect the changing everyday reality of the settlers and farmers; new places, events, and faces were commemorated in the new lyrics. Relatively simple lyrics and melodies, often utilizing repetitive lyrical and melodic devices, remained the norm, however, reflecting both the often uneducated, even illiterate, practitioners and the need for easily remembered "hooks" in a music most often learned and played by ear and transmitted by personal exposure (as opposed to recordings).

For many listeners the single most striking aspect of traditional country music is a mournful quality in both feeling and subject matter. That, too, in large part was a carryover from the folk music of the British Isles, where the agricultural poor endured lives no less precarious than they would know in North America. The older folk material was also often tinged with mystery and the supernatural, as in the timeless Scottish ballad "Barbara Allen," wherein a red rose and a briar grow from the hearts of the deceased lovers, fated by circumstance and misunderstanding never to be together in life, and tie a lovers' knot above their graves. The music of the American South would be no less permeated with death and sorrow, reflecting the seemingly eternal hard times of rural life; the often bleak outlook of the predominant religion; the region's post–Civil War history as a defeated land whose way of life had been rejected economically, morally, politically, and militarily; and the intuitive foreboding, in the face of steadily encroaching industrialization and modernization, that the way of life of the small farmer was coming to an end. "Ain't that the awfullest, morbidest song you ever heard in your life," Hank Williams, an Alabamian, said once to a journalist after singing his anguished lament "Men with Broken Hearts." "To Hank," the journalist wrote (and, he could have added, to all those who listened to and sang or played country music) "that meant it was fine. It was the highest compliment he could bestow upon his work."

Indeed, American vocal music as a whole in the decades after the Civil War tended to be death haunted; few families had been untouched by that conflict, and if the South in many ways clung to a romantic myth of the "lost cause," a sense of loss could be felt as well in the North, where a "vacant chair" was left in the parlor of many homes as remembrance of a beloved relative lost in that conflict. "Parting and death were real terrors to that generation," the historian Bernard Weisberger has written.

The exceedingly sentimental "parlor songs" of the North made their way into southern music, as did offerings from the musical stage and even some of the instruments—the mandolin, the accordion, and the Hawaiian, or steel, guitar, for example—and musical forms brought by the newer groups of immigrants who came to the United States in such large numbers between the 1840s and the 1920s. But the most important influences on the music of white southerners were exerted by those who had been unwilling immigrants to North America, whose enslavement had been the foundation of the South's rejected economic and social system and whose continued subjugation remained a cornerstone of southern society, and with whom, after the Civil War, poor whites in the South shared the land and a way of life similar in many regards: blacks.

Though clear and useful distinctions may be made between the folk music of rural southern blacks—known essentially, in its myriad permutations and facets, as the blues—and the folk music of rural southern whites—best categorized in its many aspects as country—the musical cultures of black and white southerners were never as mutually exclusive as might have been implied by the region's rigidly segregated social system. Each inevitably influenced the other. Itinerant black musicians, particularly those who sang for their living on the streets of the region's cities, had to be able to perform country material in order to please white patrons—one such wandering musician, a black street singer known only as Tee-Tot,

Jimmie Rodgers, called "the Singing Brakeman" and "the Blue Yodeler," was one of the first country stars to record with black musicians, including trumpet player Louis Armstrong, bluesman Clifford Gibson, and the Louisville Jug Band.

was young Hank Williams's musical mentor, and Bill Monroe, the inventor of bluegrass music, always cites a black neighbor, Arthur Schultz, as his single greatest musical influence—and practitioners of both musical traditions, inspired by admiration, borrowed freely from each other. The banjo, the earliest staple instrument of country music (along with the fiddle), is the descendant of a musical instrument introduced to North America by African slaves, and as country music historian Bill C. Malone explains, "the most crucial innovations in rural guitar playing came from black musicians who contributed a retinue of finger-picking styles that have forever intrigued white musicans." The guitar itself seems to have been introduced to white musicians in many parts of the South by blacks, as was its use as other than a rhythm instrument.

Indeed, the black influence on country music has been so pervasive as to be virtually impossible to separate. "Country music—seemingly the most pure white of American musical forms—has borrowed heavily from the black," Malone writes. "White southerners who would have been horrified at the idea of mixing socially with blacks . . . nonetheless enthusiastically accepted their musical offerings: the spirituals, the blues, ragtime, jazz, rhythm-and-blues, and a whole host of dance steps, vocal shadings, and instrumental techniques."

According to Frank Walker, one of the pioneers in recording Southern music, both country and the blues "came from the same area, and with the same general ideas," and white musicians often found that blues pieces went over extremely well with white audiences: one of the biggest country hits of the early days of the recording industry was "Columbus Stockade Blues" by Tom Darby and Jimmie Tarlton, one of the first recorded examples of what became known as white country blues. (Released in 1927, the record sold 200,000 copies in an era when sales of 20,000 constituted a major hit for a "hillbilly" artist; even earlier, in the 19th century, minstrel songs—musical pieces composed and performed by white musicians in conscious imitation of the music they heard performed by black musicians—had become an integral part of the white South's musical culture.) Many country musicians, despite the segregation that prevailed in virtually every aspect of country life, even recorded with black musicians, and country and blues artists were united in being considered déclassé by the (mostly) northern-based record companies that profited from their music, many of which created subsidiary labels for the recording and distribution of what they separately labeled as "race" and "old time," "hill country," "old familiar," or "hillbilly" music.

"Regardless of where they lived, in the mountains or the flatlands, the common [white] people of the South shared a passionate commitment to music," Malone wrote in his definitive history, *Country Music U.S.A.* That music was a hybrid of many influences but was reflective nonetheless of the common elements of a white, rural culture remarkably similar in its most critical components over a large geographic region. "A poor Georgian entering a small farmer's cabin in East Texas would have felt very much at home," according to Malone. "The architecture of the house, the food on the table, the dress and speech patterns of the hosts, and even the theology of the local church would have been reassuringly familiar. And more than likely there would have been a fiddle over the mantel." Before 1920 or so, that music was transmitted most often by personal exposure: southerners heard a song or musical piece that appealed to them, either in their home, played or sung by their parents, older siblings, or relatives, or at a barn dance or medicine or tent show, or in church or on a street corner, and attempted to learn or play it themselves, on a banjo, fiddle, guitar, or piano. They might alter the piece lyrically or melodically to suit their wants or abilities; in time, with enough proficiency, they might try to fashion songs or pieces of their own to reflect their own experience and concerns, perhaps using lyrics or melodies they had heard elsewhere as a base and inevitably incorporating new influences. Country musicians were not trained in any formal sense, and the songs were not often written down; feeling was more important than technique, and a heartfelt performance more valued than a technically accomplished one.

The Carter Family is seen here in the 1920s: Sara (left); A. P., Sara's husband; and Maybelle, Sara's cousin. The August 1927 recording sessions, in which the Carters and Jimmie Rodgers cut their first records in Bristol, Tennessee, Cash once said, "are the single most important event in the history of country music."

Beginning approximately in the third decade of the 20th century, new technology made it possible for the first time to disseminate such music to a mass audience. Recognizing that a market existed, executives from the fledgling recording industry in the North began making trips down south to record folk musicians. Often these sessions would take place in cities such as Dallas, Atlanta, Columbia, or Memphis, with musicians responding to what often amounted to a widely circulated general invitation to come in and lay down a couple of sides. Sometimes artist and repertory men, (A & R, as they were known), ventured farther into the field in search of authentic practitioners. One of the most important of these sessions took place in 1927 in Bristol, Tennessee, a small city in the Appalachians in the northeastern part of the state, on the border with Virginia. That session yielded the first recorded music of some of country's most important artists, most notably Jimmie Rodgers and the Carter Family, both of whom would exert a great influence on the life and music of Johnny Cash. More often, especially as the recording industry became better established, accomplished southern musicians traveled to the big cities of the North, especially New York, to cut records.

But in the 1920s records and the equipment necessary to play them were a relatively expensive investment for most Americans, and with the coming of the Great Depression the new recording industry suffered tremendously. Whereas 104 million records were sold in the United States in 1927, only 6 million were sold in 1932—a direct reflection of the hard times in the nation. With its decline, another new technology—radio— became the most important force in the dissemination of country and indeed all forms of popular music. By 1929 it was estimated that every third home in the United States had a radio in it, and in the seven preceding years sales of products advertised on the radio had climbed from $60 million to $848 million.

The 1930s thereby became, in Malone's words, "the heyday of live radio entertainment in the United States." Entrepreneurs and companies seized upon the radio as the best means of advertising their products to the consuming populace, and in the South the best means of guaranteeing a listening audience was to provide country music. Initially that music was not produced from recordings but performed live in radio studios. Country musicians traveled from place to place, from station

to station, seeking slots, most often 15 minutes in dura-
tion, in which they would perform several songs live over
the airwaves and hawk their sponsor's products. The gig
would last as long as the sponsor judged it was receiving
its money's worth, in terms of sales and cards and letters
attesting to the performer's popularity. Most professional
country musicians—an occupation made possible in
large part by the development of the recording industry
and the radio—held down several such programs at any
one time. The most desired slots, of course, were those
that traditionally attracted the largest audience: the
"farmers' hours" around sunrise, before the family had
taken to the fields, and at noon, when they broke for
dinner. Country musicians played anywhere from small
local stations to huge 50,000-watt channels that could be
heard over several states, the exposure from the radio
hopefully resulting in a demand for personal appearances.
The pinnacle of success for a country musician at that
time was a regular spot on one of the immensely popular
"barn dances," performed before large audiences and
broadcast live over large parts of the nation by the high-
powered stations on Saturday nights—such as the now-
legendary "Grand Ole Opry" from Nashville, the
"National Barn Dance" out of Chicago, the "Wheeling
Jamboree" from Wheeling, West Virginia, and the "Renfro Valley Barn Dance," performed in front of a live
audience of more than 5,000 people in tiny Renfro
Valley, Kentucky.

Even more listeners heard country music over the
so-called border radio stations. Also called X-stations,
these outfits were established just over the Mexican border to avoid U.S. broadcasting regulations governing
the size of permissible signals and could be heard
throughout much of the United States and even into
Canada. They became famous as well for the hard sell
given over their frequencies to a wide variety of products

of dubious integrity, most famously the various patent medicines and nostrums—whose main ingredients were invariably alcohol or other intoxicants—that so much of rural America, in its lack of access to and distrust of legitimate medical care, relied on as cure-alls. (One product that initially gained widespread exposure on the "National Barn Dance" is now found in most American homes: Alka-Seltzer.)

Among those listening to the music was an Arkansas farm boy named J. R. Cash. Each night, after the daily chores were done and supper was finished, he would sit by the battery-operated radio at the wooden living room table, fiddling with the knobs to bring in some mysterious, drifting, distant signal, carving nervously and absentmindedly at the table with a pocketknife. Not far away, his brother Jack sat by the kerosene lamp at the table in the dining room, where the dishes had been cleared away not long ago, reading the small print in the Bible that never left him, even when he was out in the fields. The rest of the family was in bed, Ray and Carrie retiring without fail each night at 8:05, after the news came over the airwaves.

Decades later, those nights with the radio remained vivid to Johnny Cash. He still remembered the call letters of the stations, the far-off sounding names of the cities they broadcast from, the names of the musicians, and the way, each night without fail, his father would shout at his boys to "blow out the light" and go to bed. "The later it got, the lower I had to turn the radio because I didn't want Daddy to know I was still up," he said. "I'd sit and listen with my ear against the radio and my pocketknife in my hand, just whittling. I was nervous 'cause I knew Daddy was fixing at any minute to holler for me to go to bed. . . . 'All right,' he'd yell. 'Get up and turn that radio off and go to bed. You're not gonna want to get up in the morning.' I can hear him saying it now, just as plain.

I never sat there at night and listened to that radio that Daddy didn't say it."

And he never sat there that he did not stay up just a little bit longer, to hear one more song, one last song: "I had to hear those songs. Nothing in the world was as important to me as hearing those songs on the radio. The music carried me above the mud, the work, and the hot sun. . . . I'd turn it down a little and get my ear closer in. . . . I remember I could turn that dial and pick up WLW in New Orleans, and WCKY in Cincinnati, and KOMA in Oklahoma City, WJJD in Chicago, or XEG in Fort Worth. And XERF in Del Rio, Texas. I heard all those Carter Family transcriptions they had broadcast on

The Alabamian Hank Williams performs on the "Grand Ole Opry" program, broadcast Saturday nights on Nashville's WSM radio station. After appearing on the "Grand Ole Opry," Williams, whose songs "Cold, Cold Heart" and "I'm So Lonesome I Could Cry" are classics, became one of the most popular country music stars of all time.

XERF. . . . And every night at six o'clock from WJJD in Chicago, we all listened to Suppertime Frolics. It was country songs and hymns and jokes. . . . Every Saturday night there would be the Grand Ole Opry from WSM in Nashville. And I'd listen too to the Renfro Valley Barn Dance and to the Wheeling Jamboree on WWVA from Wheeling, West Virginia. . . . I thought they were playing those songs just for me."

Sometimes the family would make its own music. Ray would play the piano, and Carrie and all the children would harmonize, usually on hymns. (Years later Johnny Cash would have a number one hit with his friend Carl Perkins's musical remembrance of his own family's

similar harmonizing, "Daddy Sang Bass.") When Roy Cash, who was by now living in Blytheville, formed a group that would sometimes practice at the Cash home, J. R. was astonished and pleased to discover that his mother, the daughter of a singing teacher, could play each one of the band's instruments—fiddle, banjo, guitar, and harmonica. Surprisingly though, his mother's first attempt to encourage his obvious interest in music did not take. She bought J. R. an inexpensive guitar from the *Sears, Roebuck Catalogue* and tried to teach him to play, but he was too impatient to learn and ultimately sold the instrument to a neighbor.

Of the Cash children, no two were closer than Jack and J. R. "Jack was my protector," Johnny wrote in *The Man in Black*. "I was the skinny one, and he looked after me. We were always together, always laughing. He taught me all those things a big brother teaches a little brother he loves. There was nobody in the world as good and as wise and as strong as my big brother Jack."

One Saturday morning in early May 1944, the two had a good-natured disagreement as to how they were going to spend their day. J. R. wanted his big brother to go fishing with him at a favorite spot on one of the drainage ditches, but Jack felt obligated, despite a vague apprehension that he expressed to both his brother and his mother, to spend the day cutting fence posts at the school's agriculture shop, for which he would be paid $3 that the family could use. So the two brothers walked together for a mile on their way to their individual pursuits, then split up at a fork in the road, each to go their own way.

Two hours later, J. R. was heading back home. It was hot and humid, and the fish were lying low; he had not even had a nibble. At the fork in the road, "along came my father with the preacher in a black car," the clergy-man's Model A Ford. "Jack's been hurt awfully bad," Ray Cash finally managed to say after his son got in the car, and J. R. immediately knew that the truth was even worse than his father could bring himself to say, for, he later recalled, "I'd never seen Daddy like that." At home Ray brought J. R. out to the smokehouse and laid Jack's bloody clothes out on the floor; "the pants and shirt were cut from the bottom of the rib cage down to the pelvis, and the belt was sliced in two." Somehow Jack had been jerked into or fallen onto a circular saw, and it had laid him open right down the middle. "You can see how bad he's been hurt," Ray Cash said. "I'm afraid I'm going to lose him." Then he began—the only time his third son would know him to do so—to cry. His boy stumbled outside and sank down on a woodpile, unable to stand.

A doctor operated, but there was nothing that could be done. Jack lingered for more than a week, alternately lucid and delirious, before dying. "He knew he was gonna die," his brother would later say. "He was only fourteen, but he was as much a man in his thinking and acting as anyone I ever knew." J. R. was there at the end; "Goodbye, Jack," was all he could bring himself to say, while his brother spoke aloud of a river he could see, with "fire on one side and heaven on the other," and of the "beautiful city" he was about to enter, and asked his mother if she could hear the singing angels that he could hear. "I wish you could hear the angels singing," he said again and again, and then he passed. "My grief would be a long time going," Johnny Cash would later say, and not long afterward he wrote his first songs.

4 ★ I Walk the Line

AFTER JACK'S DEATH J. R. grew more introverted and restless than ever. "He thought more and talked even less," his sister Reba recalls. He was shocked by the recognition that a tragedy of such magnitude had left the world unchanged. Everyone who attended the funeral at the First Baptist Church agreed that they had never seen so many people in one place, but the day after the funeral the sun still came up early and set late, the cotton still needed chopping, and the animals still had to be fed. In only one way did the world seem aware of what had happened: "It rained a lot that spring," Johnny Cash remembered.

J. R. kept his pain inside. He said little, but sang—in a high tenor voice that carried, he later said, for miles across the fields—all the time, especially while working his daddy's land, revealing a rare gift for musical and lyrical recall that enabled him to master and repeat songs he had heard just once. For all his reticence, he revealed himself also to be quick with words, in the form of song lyrics he would make up on the spot to entertain his friends and poems that he would later set to music. "There were love songs, sad songs,"

A movie still from *Road to Nashville* (1966) captures the deep-set dark eyes and somber mien of Johnny Cash.

he later said. "I think the death of my brother . . . had a lot to do with it." The radio continued to be as important to him as eating and breathing, with Roy Acuff, the leading light of the "Grand Ole Opry"; the deceased but eternally popular Jimmie Rodgers; the "Texas Troubador,"

Ernest Tubb; and (especially after 1948) Hank Williams being particular heroes.

A somewhat less well-known duo, the Louvin Brothers—Ira, who played the mandolin and sang tenor, and Charlie, who played the guitar and sang baritone—were

Roy Acuff (with fiddle) and his Smoky Mountain Boys perform "Wabash Cannonball" on WSM's "Grand Old Opry" in 1943. J. R. soaked up the songs he heard on the radio and was able to sing them verbatim even after listening to them only once.

71

In 1947 J. R. attended a show by country music's Louvin Brothers at Dyess High School. Cash later recalled thinking to himself after their performance, "I'll be up there someday. That's what I'm gonna be."

also special favorites; they sang, with their characteristic intricate, pure, high, lonesome harmonies, secular songs each day from 12:30 to 1:00 as part of the "High Noon Roundup" over WMPS from Memphis, and 15 minutes of gospel at 1:00. The family always returned to the fields from its noontime dinner at one o'clock, but J. R. was invariably allowed an extra quarter of an hour to listen to the Louvins. In 1947 they even played a show at the Dyess County High School. J. R. Cash was there two hours early to watch them arrive, in the biggest car he had ever seen—"I suppose it was a limousine, though I'd never heard of one at that time"—and he was the only one left in the lot outside the auditorium when they pulled away, thinking to himself, he later wrote, "I'll be up there someday. That's what I'm gonna be." When Charlie Louvin returned his farewell wave, the thrill was as great, J. R. said, as when he had been a three-year-old boy watching a train rumble through and the engineer waved down at him, or even tooted the whistle. "But then Charlie Louvin couldn't really help but notice me," he wrote. "I was the only one left at the auditorium standing at that single light outside the stage door. I watched the taillights on that limousine disappear down the dirt road, and then I started home."

With no real choice, the family went on and found certain consolations for Jack's death. Carrie Cash took some solace in J. R.'s emerging musical talent, which she considered a legacy handed on from her own father, who had "led the singing" at the Crossroads Methodist Church for 40 years. In looks, too, J. R. reminded her of her daddy, and it was clear that he was going to be tall like him as well. When the boy turned 16, she started taking in laundry to earn extra money to pay for voice lessons for him. The lessons lasted only a month, however; after hearing him sing "Lovesick Blues," Hank Williams's breakthrough hit, the teacher confessed that there was little she could teach him; the rest was up to him and the Lord.

One day not long after, as J. R. came in from the fields after a day spent chopping wood with his father, he was singing to himself as he walked in the back door—a not uncommon sound in the household, but one that on this day, according to *The Man in Black,* made his mother wheel quickly around. "Who was that singing in such a low, booming voice?" she demanded to know. "That was me," J. R. said. He was, he later wrote, "almost as surprised as she." Gone was the high tenor of his adolescence, replaced with a cavernous bass that in a few short years would make him famous. "You sound exactly like my daddy," Carrie Cash said tearfully, as her son experimented with just how deep his new voice could go. "I don't know exactly what He has in mind, but God has His hand on you."

But there was little his talent could do for him in Dyess, and very little there now to hold him. Electricity had come to the colony in 1946, and his father added 20 more acres to his spread and even bought a (13-year-old) car, but by the time J. R. graduated from high school in 1950, Ray Cash had leased out his land (he would sell soon thereafter) and had taken a job at the Procter &

Gamble oleomargarine plant in nearby Evadale, where he had quickly worked his way up to foreman. So without the land to hold him, and without a sweetheart to make him think twice about leaving, J. R. Cash did what so many young men from the South were doing in those days: he lit out north for the plentiful work and steady wages to be found in the automobile factories in and around Detroit, Michigan.

He lasted less than a month. Though he returned home "with more money than I ever had in my life," the job—lifting hoods onto automobile chassis on the assembly line in the Fisher auto body plant in Pontiac, a Detroit suburb—had been "sheer drudgery," and Detroit "like a foreign country" to him. "It wasn't my kind of work, and it wasn't my kind of people," he later told an interviewer, adding that he had often been insulted because of his background, referred to as "country boy," "hillbilly," or "hick." He tried his hand at the oleomargarine plant, but that, too, lasted only a couple of weeks. Out of work, more restless than ever, truly interested only in one thing but lacking the confidence to try to make a living at it, he exercised another common option of southern boys looking for a way to get off the land: he enlisted in the armed services—specifically, the U.S. Air Force.

Though not eager for combat—the United States had just become involved in the Korean War—Cash nevertheless quickly earned the attention and admiration of his superior officers. Upon completion of his basic training, he had no trouble deciding between the various duty choices offered him: there was little doubt that John Cash, as he was now

In the 1940s, students in the U.S. Army Flying School attend a radio class. After Cash completed basic training in the U.S. Air Force, he was offered duty as a radio operator. He excelled in training and was selected for top secret missions to Italy and other political hot spots.

known, would choose to become a radio operator. In the six months of intensive training that followed, the characteristic that virtually everyone who knows this relatively uneducated country boy always mentions—his intelligence—came to the fore, and Cash finished the course four weeks ahead of all the other trainees. His prowess so impressed his instructors that he was chosen as a candidate for the U.S. Air Force Security Service, which monitors international radio traffic, particularly, at that time, the communications of the Soviet Union. Again, Cash excelled in the training sessions, which took place at Brooks Air Force Base near San Antonio, Texas, outperforming the many college graduates who had been selected for the program and earning an assignment to Landberg, West Germany (now Germany), an important cold war listening post. He also dated, for three short weeks before leaving for Europe, Vivian Liberto, a 17-year-old high school senior whom he had met at a roller-skating rink in San Antonio.

Cash would later characterize his time in the service as "four long, miserable years," but he was not always unhappy. In Landberg he quickly proved himself one of the most talented of the Security Service's radio intercept operators, the one who was always called upon for the most difficult assignments, and the work gave him a sense of pride and accomplishment. He was "proud of it," he later said, because he "excelled at it."

Even more important to him were the friendships he made: several young men from rural southern backgrounds like his own, all of them amateur country musicians. In the barracks in off-duty hours they assembled an informal group, the Landberg Barbarians, and sang and played the music of Hank Williams, Ernest Tubb, Hank Snow, Jimmie Rodgers, the Carter Family, and others, including some of their own compositions. Encouraged by them, Cash bought his first guitar (for

$4.80) and learned a few chords, then purchased a tape recorder and began working on his own numbers.

He even had the lyrics to one of his songs, "Hey, Porter," printed as a poem in the base newspaper. He also developed for the first time a taste for beer and stronger alcoholic drinks.

In Dyess, said a friend, "J. R. weren't no angel, but [he] never did get in no meanness [he] couldn't get out of." Now, however, he began to engage in some serious hell-raising, giving up church and chapel services in favor of taverns and three-day binges when he had passes. "I got to where I loved that beer in Germany," he said. "I'd go out and try to get a fight started." His antics were tolerated because of his skill as a radio operator, and he actually earned several promotions; by the time of his honorable discharge in July 1954 at the end of his tour of duty, he had attained the rank of staff sergeant.

He returned, his mother immediately noticed, more taciturn, high-strung, and "edgy" than ever. He spoke to no one about his worries, as usual, but his family was certain they knew: the service had been only a holding action, and his future seemed no brighter, his possibilities no less limited. And he had new responsibilities now: one month after his return, on August 7, 1954, he and Vivian Liberto were married; the first of their four daughters, Roseanne, was born just over nine months later.

They settled in Memphis, Tennessee, where his brother Roy, who worked as a mechanic for a Chevrolet dealership, found him a job as an appliance salesman for Home Equipment, a position for which he proved spectacularly unsuited. His bluntness and honesty did not serve him well: most of his sales calls were supposed to be made in the poorest neighborhoods of Memphis, and Cash felt uncomfortable about selling the residents of such areas overpriced, secondhand refrigerators and washing machines. "I hated every minute of it," he re-

called in later years. "I'd go down to the poorest sections of town, but I might as well have told them, 'You don't want to buy anything anyway.' I'd be in a home and see a guitar, and I'd sit and play and forget the business." After a while he stopped even making calls; instead he would sit in his car and listen to the radio. But daydreaming did not pay the bills, and he worked on commission. On weekends he would go back to Dyess, where his mother interpreted his brooding silences. "He wasn't selling enough to live on," she remembered; "he realized he wasn't doing any good, but he kept his troubles to himself."

In October 1966, Cash poses with his wife, Vivian, and their daughters. Cash had met Vivian Liberto at a skating rink in Texas when he was in the air force; they married after he completed his term of duty in 1954.

There was a brighter side, of course. His landlady, Pat Isom, forgave his frequent delinquencies with the rent; she took a liking to him when she went to Home Equipment to buy a refrigerator and he told her the model she contemplated buying was not worth the price. Aside from money worries, he was happy at home and felt no compulsion to resume the rowdy ways he had learned in Germany. His brother Roy introduced him to two mechanics down at the garage, Marshall Grant and Luther Perkins, and the three men began getting together in their spare time to strum guitars and sing country songs; they even played a couple of local gigs and a 15-minute program of gospel music over KWEM radio each Saturday, sponsored by George Bates, Cash's boss at Home Equipment, who felt sorry for his hapless salesman. And most fortunate of all, he was in Memphis, which, although it did not appear to him at the moment to be the land of opportunity, was in fact at the eye of a musical storm that was about to transform America.

By the mid-1950s Nashville, the state capital of Tennessee, was firmly established as the center of the country music industry, well on its way to earning its self-proclaimed reputation as "Music City, U.S.A." The Grand Ole Opry was still there, of course, and was still the single most important country music venue, as were the most up-to-date recording studios and the slickest, tightest, most adept studio musicians, the famed Nashville Cats. But the sound of records made in Nashville tended to be homogenized, syrupy, comparatively sophisticated, almost pop, with much of the rough edges of country music's most authentic practitioners smoothed out. By the end of the decade, a typical Nashville record would be heavily orchestrated, almost invariably featuring strings and sugary, overdubbed backing vocals.

Country music was by then very big business, and record executives, particularly from the big labels such as

Decca, Capitol, Victor, Columbia, and RCA, were constantly looking for ways to "cross over" and reach the pop audience. The formulaic music then being made in Nashville, sometimes referred to as "country pop" or "countrypolitan," was consciously crafted to reach as broad an audience as possible, resulting in the sacrifice of the most traditional and distinctive elements of the country style. Even so, it was generally assumed that any performer with an aspiration of making it big in country music would sooner or later make his or her way to Nashville.

The scene in Memphis, several hundred miles to the southwest, had a completely different feel to it. Nashville is the capital of Tennessee, an old adage has it, but Memphis is the capital of Mississippi. Another old saw puts it a different way: The Mississippi Delta begins just outside the lobby of the Commodore Hotel (a longtime Memphis landmark). As a Mississippi river city dependent on traffic in agricultural commerce, Memphis has traditionally seemed more vitally connected with, and more a part of, the Deep South states below it—Mississippi and Arkansas—than with the rest of the state; and as a result its musical culture unavoidably reflects the influence of the Mississippi Delta, the heartland of the blues. Black music of all kinds—blues, jazz, and the new hybrid called rhythm and blues—had long thrived in Memphis, especially in the juke joints and dives along Beale Street, the legendary main drag of the city's black section.

Of course, as in any southern city at that time, country music was always popular in Memphis; as the major urban center for the Mississippi Delta, the city had always attracted young whites off the farm, like John Cash, and they brought their music with them. The result, on the airwaves and in the small recording studios of Memphis, was an intoxicating blend of styles and sounds perhaps not found anywhere else in the country. It could be heard to best effect on such radio broadcasts as the celebrated and immensely popular "Red Hot and Blue" program hosted by the illustrious disc jockey Dewey Phillips, a revolutionary in his own way, who played country, blues, jazz, pop—whatever appealed to him, without regard to category or race.

The many young aspiring musicians in the city, or within range of its radio stations, could not help but be influenced. Whenever he had money left over from one of his infrequent appliance sales, John Cash haunted the famous Home of the Blues record store, looking for discs by such artists as Delta bluesmen Robert Johnson and Howlin' Wolf, black "songster" Pink Anderson, or black gospel singer Rosetta Tharpe. His all-time favorite album, he would later say, is *Blues in the Mississippi Night,* a haunting session, recorded in the late 1940s by the

Cash frequently patronized Memphis's Home of the Blues record store (far right), buying discs of Howlin' Wolf, Robert Johnson, and Rosetta Tharpe, among others.

Bluesmen Little Bill Gaither (left), Memphis Slim, and Big Bill Broonzy were a few of Cash's favorite musicians. Cash once said that every successful country singer has black blues as part of his or her heritage.

distinguished musical folklorist Alan Lomax, of musical performances and spoken reminiscences by the eminent bluesmen Memphis Slim, Big Bill Broonzy, and the original Sonny Boy Williamson. When making sales calls for Home Equipment, he planned each day so that he would end up in Orange Mound, a black shantytown where he befriended many blues musicians, especially Gus Cannon, an old banjo player and songwriter. This belated exposure to black music, Cash would come to feel, was the much needed final lesson in his musical education. "Every successful country singer I know," he would say in 1968 to music critic Robert Shelton, "has a humble background, beginning, and the [black] blues have been a part of their musical heritage. Every one of them, bar none."

At the center of this musical ferment was a young radio announcer named Sam Phillips, sole proprietor of the nondescript storefront recording studio at 706 Union Avenue in Memphis that was home to Sun Records. As music journalist Colin Escott has written, "the notion that a record label of national importance could emerge from Memphis would have been—in fact, was—laughed at in 1950," but Phillips had big dreams. An intriguing mix of idealism and calculation, he believed that Sun Records could nudge its way into the big time by recording material that the major labels mostly ignored: "race"—that is, black—music and more authentic, energetic representations of country music than were coming out of Nashville. Phillips had spent the first years of his childhood on a farm in Alabama, where he had cultivated a love for both blues and country music; in the best of both forms, he believed, was an emotional urgency and honesty of expression that was missing from most popular music of the day and that people would respond to.

"There were two types of downtrodden people back then," Phillips said of his childhood. "There were the black field hands and the white sharecroppers. It was impossible in those days not to hear and grow to love all the music of oppression and the music that uplifted people—blues, country, gospel, all of it." Years later, in 1950, he opened his studio "with the intention of recording singers and musicians from Memphis and the locality who I felt had something that people should be able to hear. I'm talking about blues—both the country style and rhythm style—and also about gospel or spiritual music and white country music. I always felt that people who played this type of music had not been given the opportunity to reach an audience. I feel strongly that a lot of the blues was a real true story. Unadulterated life as it was . . . My aim was to try and record the blues and other music I liked and to prove whether I was right or wrong about this music. I knew, or *felt* I knew, that there was a bigger audience for blues than just the black man of the mid-South. There were city markets to be reached, and I knew that whites listened to blues surreptitiously."

By 1954 Phillips had experienced some artistic success but had reaped only extremely limited financial rewards. He had recorded some of the first sides laid down by a blues guitar prodigy named B. B. King and a minor hit, "Rocket 88," by a black rhythm and blues combo featuring Ike Turner on piano, that he would later characterize as the first true rock and roll record. He had even captured on disc for the first time the powerful, unsurpassed blues artistry of Howlin' Wolf (Chester Burnett), who was, Phillips would always maintain, the single greatest talent he ever worked with. "When I heard him," he recalled several decades after that shattering experience, "I said, 'This is for me. This is where the soul of man never dies.' . . . He sang with his damn soul. . . . He had no voice in the sense of a pretty voice but he had command of every word he spoke."

Despite these and other breakthroughs, Sun Records was barely breaking even, and Phillips believed he knew the reason why: racism and fear made whites generally reluctant to buy or listen to records made by black musicians. "If I could find," he is supposed to have said, "a white boy who could sing like a Negro, I could make me a million dollars." Though the quote may be apocryphal, there is no doubt that Phillips was looking for someone—of necessity, someone white—who could present the feel of the black music he loved in a way that white audiences would not find threatening. And then, in May or June 1954, that man walked through the door of 706 Union Avenue.

Actually, over the next two years, three such men came in to record at Sun. It was perhaps inevitable that some of the young musicians around Memphis—those who listened to Dewey Phillips on the radio or grew up hearing the type of music that Sam Phillips had and loved it in the same way—would wind up with a similar idea: to marry the more insistent rhythms of black music to country-type material, or even to sing black material themselves in their own way, not in slavish imitation, but preserving the feel. None of them had made the same kind of commercial calculation as Phillips had; without exception they were all young, completely inexperienced in the music business. They had simply, independently, without much conscious thought about it, put together the kinds of music they liked and created something new. None of them was responding to Phillips's direction; their ideas and styles were largely formed before they walked into Sun. Phillips's genius was in recognizing the originality of their talents and allowing it to express itself. Together, these country boys invented nothing less than rock and roll.

The first (and most important) was a handsome young Memphis truck driver named Elvis Presley. "Here's ol' Elvis," Phillips used to say jokingly to the aspiring singer, who liked to hang around the studio, "coming to see what kind of star we can make of him today." Presley tried his hand at a couple of country-type ballads, and although Phillips liked his voice, he did not see anything special there—until one day in July 1954, when Elvis and his backing musicians, bassist Bill Black and guitarist Scotty Moore, began fooling around with a high-energy version of "That's All Right, Mama," which had been a minor hit as a race record for bluesman Arthur "Big Boy" Crudup.

What Phillips heard affected him in just the same way Presley's new sound and hip-swiveling live performances would, in a very short time, affect the rest of the nation. "That's All Right, Mama" would be Presley's first single; on the flip side he recorded a rollicking version of Bill Monroe's classic bluegrass lament, "Blue Moon of Kentucky." Though Presley would sometimes claim that he had just "stumbled upon" the sound that rocked America, in 1956 he was more articulate and forthright about the roots of his music: "The colored folks been singing it and playing it just like I'm doing it now, man, for more years than I know. . . . They played it like that in the shanties and juke joints, and nobody paid it no mind till I goosed it up. I got it from them. Down in Tupelo, Mississippi, I used to hear old Arthur Crudup bang his box the way I do now, and I said if I ever got to the place I could feel what old Arthur felt, I'd be a music man like nobody ever saw."

The single caused a sensation in the Memphis market-place and earned Presley a spot, just 12 weeks after his career began—an unprecedented honor for a new artist—on the "Grand Ole Opry," where, however, his hard-driving sound and freewheeling vocals were not particularly well received. "That's not country," the elders of the Opry grumbled; "go back to driving a truck." Over the next year or so Presley would cut eight more sides for Sun; the last, "Mystery Train," a cover of a rhythm and blues number Phillips had recorded, backed with an up-tempo version of "I Forgot To Remember To Forget," a country weeper, made it to number one in the country charts. Presley was well on his way to becoming the biggest sensation in the history of American music, and a new, hybrid musical form—rock and roll—would soon rule the airwaves.

Seventeen months after "That's All Right, Mama," Sun released "Blue Suede Shoes," by a guitar player and singer named Carl Perkins, who had grown up on a sharecropper's cotton farm in Lake County, Tennessee, just across the Mississippi from the Cash place in Arkansas. "Perkins had this feel for *pushing* a song along that very few people had," Phillips said. "I knew that Carl could rock and in fact he told me right from the start that he had been playing that music before Elvis came out on record." Perkins himself described his own style as relatively simple, based on ideas similar to Presley's: "I just speeded up some of the slow blues licks. . . . That's all. That's what rockabilly music or rock 'n' roll was to begin with: a country man's song with a black man's rhythm."

Rock and roller Jerry Lee Lewis reels atop a grand piano during a New York performance in 1958. Lewis helped Sun Records' Sam Phillips attain his dream of crossover hits with "Great Balls of Fire," which reached the top of the country and R & B charts.

"Blue Suede Shoes" was an even bigger sensation than any of Presley's Sun sides had been. The label's first million-seller, it became the first record in history to reach the national pop, country, and rhythm and blues charts.

From Ferriday, Louisiana, then came the Killer, the wildest and perhaps most talented of all the Sun "rockabillies," 21-year-old, uneducated, twice-married, once-jailed, perpetually broke, peroxide blond Jerry Lee Lewis, who had heard Elvis's records and concluded that perhaps Phillips might be the man to appreciate his manic, keyboard-driven, idiosyncratic meld of musical idioms, which had earned him only the cold shoulder in Nashville. Lewis's raucous, piano-thumping Sun singles "Whole Lotta Shaking Going On" and "Great Balls of Fire" would both reach the top of the national country and rhythm and blues charts. Phillips had succeeded in surpassing Nashville's wildest crossover dreams, and American music would never be the same.

Presley, Perkins, and Lewis constituted three-quarters of what became known as Sun's Million Dollar Quartet. The fourth member was Johnny Cash, who with Marshall Grant and Luther Perkins had finally, after numerous tries, prevailed upon Phillips to let them cut a few sides on March 22, 1955. Cash had wanted to record some gospel and religious songs, but Phillips explained that there was no market for such material, and they recorded instead two songs that Cash had written, one in Germany and one more recently—"Hey, Porter," a homesick southern boy's rhythmic lament as he rides the rails back to Dixie, and "Folsom Prison Blues," the song of a convict inspired to dream of freedom by the sound of a train coming around the bend. Phillips liked the first but not the second, which Cash sang in an unnaturally high voice far removed from his usual rumbling bass, and sent him home to write another song. He returned two months later with "Cry, Cry, Cry," about a faithless woman whose rambling ways are sure to lead to heartache. With "Hey, Porter," it became the first record by Johnny Cash and the Tennessee Two.

By most accounts it was Phillips who persuaded Cash to call himself Johnny, convincing him that it would be more appealing to the youth market, although Vivian Liberto Cash has said that he introduced himself to her as Johnny Cash. The singer himself initially wanted to call his group the Tennessee Three—none of the trio was actually from the state—but his sidemen urged him to take top billing, perhaps because the whole enterprise seemed to be so much more important to him than it was to them. "Even at this stage," said bassist Marshall Grant, "making a career of it was the farthest thing from my mind and Luther's, because we were already making good salaries. I'm sure it was in John's mind because he wasn't making any money."

"I don't know these boys," Grant heard Sleepy-Eyed John, a popular Memphis disc jockey, say over the air on June 21, 1955, the day the single was released, "but I've never heard anything come in with such a different sound. It won't be the last you've heard of them." The single went right to number one on the Memphis country charts and to number fourteen nationally.

Six months later, Cash's second record—a rerecorded version of "Folsom Prison Blues" backed with "So Doggone Lonesome," another original composition—was released and shot up immediately to number four on the national country charts. It earned enough money for him to quit his job at Home Equipment and take the band out on the road more or less full-time in his green 1954 Plymouth. They played one-night gigs everywhere from Georgia to Colorado and Arizona, with a weekly 750-mile commute from Memphis to Shreveport, Louisiana, every Saturday night to appear on the "Louisiana

Hayride," a live barn dance show, known as the "cradle of the stars," where Hank Williams and Elvis had received some of their first national exposure. Many of these appearances were on packages with the other Sun "rock-abillies," as Presley, Perkins, Lewis, and their scores of imitators were soon dubbed.

Although, as journalist Arthur Levy has observed, Cash "seemed much more country than those famed labelmates who completed the Million Dollar Quartet," he clearly contributed to and benefited from the new thing that was happening in music. More rhythmically driven than the other country music being recorded at the time, Cash's sound, in the absence of the lush orna-mentation of Nashville records, was at once both modern and traditional, a throwback to the more rugged and spare sounds of older, folk-based country music (as op-posed to the commercial product) and right in step with the even more hopped-up music of Elvis and the others. It was a sound arrived at more out of necessity than calculation; Phillips remembers Cash in the early days being most apologetic about the group's technical short-comings, and Marshall Grant admitted that "we didn't work to get that 'boom-chicka-boom' sound. That's all we could play." Indeed, the group's instrumental lineup, with Luther Perkins on electric guitar and Grant on stand-up bass, which Cash had suggested—previously, all three had played acoustic guitars—had only been in place a little while when they went into the studio to record for the first time. Grant admits to having played the bass less than two dozen times before recording "Hey, Porter," and it took the group some 35 takes to get the relatively simple "Cry, Cry, Cry."

For Phillips, such technical limitations were in fact virtues. He knew that music listeners, particularly young listeners, were looking for something more elemental than the quasi-sophisticated pop and country songs they

Johnny Cash (center) and the Tennessee Two (Luther Perkins, left, on guitar and Marshall Grant, right, on bass) perform at the Grand Ole Opry while Roy Acuff dances to the music.

were being fed, and he recognized that the instrumental sound of Cash and the Tennessee Two was, for all its seeming primitiveness, as absolutely distinctive as Cash's voice. "I didn't want anything to detract from the command that Johnny had with just the sound of his voice," Phillips said, so instead of embellishing his instrumental accompaniment, he simply emphasized the spare sound of the Tennessee Two and Cash's acoustic guitar, using a slight echo, placing the vocals more out front in the mix than was common at the time, and enhancing the rhythm—Cash says it was actually his idea—by placing a piece of paper between the guitar strings and the neck, which gave something of the effect of a drummer playing with brushes.

And though Cash, then as now, considered himself to be a country artist, he—unlike many others in the country music establishment—saw nothing sacrilegious in the new variant that Presley, Lewis, and Perkins were creating. Indeed, he wrote "Get Rhythm"—which, with another of his compositions, "I Walk the Line," would be his third Sun record—for Presley, and gave Perkins the idea for "Blue Suede Shoes." Onstage he lacked none of the charisma of his more flamboyant labelmates, reaching an audience not with Presley's hip-shaking ecstasy or Lewis's piano-thumping madness but with his voice and a presence that Grant had noticed the first time he met him: "Before I ever shook his hand, before I ever spoke to him, I saw him coming down the rows of cars, and he seemed almost magnetic. Even though he was just J. R. then, there was something that caught your attention. He was tall and dark, and he was edgy as a cat on a tin roof." Whereas Presley and Lewis let it all hang out onstage, whipping up their audiences into a frenzy that was clearly sexual, there was about Cash something always moody and reserved, but no less attractive. Like the brooding movie stars of that era who would appeal to the same young audience that was responding to rock and roll—Montgomery Clift, Marlon Brando, and James Dean—Cash seemed always to be holding something back; there was an air of loneliness and mystery about him, even in these years before he started wearing only black onstage. "When I first got up on the stage of the Grand Ole Opry, with my black clothes and sideburns, they didn't know what I was," he remembered years later.

If Elvis and Jerry Lee tempted youngsters with the forbidden fruit of sexual desire, there was something even darker, more dangerous in the rebellion at the core of Cash's music, as exemplified in "Folsom Prison Blues." Outlaws have always been staple characters in country music, but the narrator of Cash's song is a different breed entirely. The many outlaws and imprisoned men in country music had been of two kinds: either Robin Hood figures, champions of the common man, such as (in song) Jesse James and Pretty Boy Floyd, driven justifiably outside the law by injustice on the part of the rich and powerful or their representatives; or those who, by succumbing (most commonly by ignoring the advice and love of their mother) to the temptations and vices of the fast life or the big city, in the form of drink, cards, and women, wind up on the wrong side of the law and sing their song as an act of repentance for their headstrong ways and misdeeds, thereby reaffirming the verities of home, family, and the rural life.

But Cash's bad man had no excuses, and he was not very sorry either. His mother had taught him as a child to "always be a good boy" and never "play with guns," but he "shot a man in Reno just to watch him die." Though the sound of the "lonesome" train whistle makes him cry in his jail cell, his tears are not shed, as they would be in a more traditional country ballad, for any of his own misdeeds, for anyone he has hurt, for fear for his immortal soul, or even for missing his home and family; though he perfunctorily acknowledges that he "[has] it coming," the real cause of his blues is not guilt or remorse but the knowledge that the train is free to roll on and he is not.

In this short song, which contains, like virtually all of his compositions, no choruses, Cash assembles several of the most common elements of country song—a solicitous mother; a wayfaring, straying son; a train; and a murder—but reaches a conclusion quite different from what the traditions of the form would have dictated: the killing is unjustified, even by the killer's own logic, and the killer without remorse, yet the listener is expected to identify with his plight. Where in country songs the railroad had often served as a double-edged symbol of progress and freedom—it offered a means for men to indulge their "rough and rowdy ways," as Jimmie Rodgers famously put it. Those who rode away from the land on the iron horse, however, usually came to regret it, and it brought the temptations of the big city that much closer—in Cash's composition the train is an unambiguous vehicle of deliverance for one who cannot lay a deserving claim to it. And if freed, the unrepentant killer intends not to return to his loved ones—indeed, there is no sign that he even has any, for the song provides no indication of any emotional attachment, either way, between himself and his mother—but to continue his rambling, to "move it on a little farther down the line."

Released in April 1956, "I Walk the Line" became Cash's first crossover hit, reaching number one in the national country charts and number seventeen on the pop side. A hypnotically simple pledge of fidelity, with a hummed two-bar break between each verse that announces a descent into a lower register, the song remains Cash's all-time best-seller and was his breakthrough to national prominence. In its wake he received a 10-show guest spot on the "Jackie Gleason Show" (Elvis had gotten only five appearances), made numerous appearances on other television shows, secured a permanent slot on the "Grand Ole Opry," and played to ever larger audiences in every state of the union. But to Cash, looking back, "those weren't the good old days."

5 ★ Ring of Fire

PHILLIPS'S PROBLEM, obviously, was not recognizing talent but hanging on to it; he could have used a little luck as well. In late 1955 continuing financial difficulties forced him to put Presley's contract up for sale, and the "hillbilly cat" left Sun. Early the next year Carl Perkins, who was then the hottest act in the country, with "Blue Suede Shoes" holding steady in the pop, country, and R & B charts just ahead of "Heartbreak Hotel," Elvis's first RCA release, was badly injured in an automobile accident while traveling to New York to make what would have been the first national network television appearance by a rock and roller; his career would never regain its lost momentum. In the spring of 1958 scandal brought down Jerry Lee Lewis, who was then at the top of the charts, when the press revealed that his new bride, Myra Friedman, was not yet 14 years old. She "might look young and is young but is growed," Lewis said, but the reports seemed to confirm everything rock and roll's many opponents were saying about its dangerous libidinal influences, and Lewis was blacklisted from the top forty. And in August of that same year, Johnny Cash left Sun for Columbia Records.

"Big River," "Home of the Blues," and "Give My Love to Rose" became big sellers for Cash and Sun Records. In 1958, however, he left Sun for Columbia Records, which offered a bigger share of the profits from his hits.

Cash's Sun work had continued to chart well, and most of it stands up as the best of his career. Indeed, in the opinion of Colin Escott, "he never sounded quite as good as he had on his earliest recordings," and in 1994 Cash remained justifiably proud of his groundbreaking Sun sides. "I was never part of the country music establishment, churning out hits for the country Top 40," he told an interviewer for MTV. "My peers are Jerry Lee Lewis, Carl Perkins, and Elvis." Two of those Sun sides would reach number one on the country charts, the rather silly "Ballad of a Teenage Queen" and the marvelously stoic "Guess Things Happen That Way," and everything else released on the label before his departure—"Don't Make Me Go," "Next in Line," "Train of Love," "There You Go," "Big River," "Give My Love to Rose," and "Home of the Blues"—would all perform superbly well. The last three, especially, qualify for any list of Cash classics. "Big River," inspired by a magazine article that said "Johnny Cash has the big river blues in his voice" but written far from that source in the unlikely setting of White Plains, New York, contains some of his best writing, including the immortal opening line, "I taught the weeping willow how to cry, cry, cry"; it received new life and a new listening audience in the 1970s when it was recorded by the Grateful Dead. The mournful "Home of the Blues," the title of which was inspired by the Memphis record store of the same name, represents Cash's first experiment with a fuller instrumental sound than that provided by the Tennessee Two, and features one of his most affecting vocals. "Give My Love to Rose," a sentimental ballad about a dying ex-convict's last wish, written by the singer in a club 10 blocks from San Quentin prison, is simply vintage Cash.

Even so, Cash was frustrated both financially and artistically at Sun. Phillips might have been able to sell more records than some of the major labels, but his business was not yet in good enough shape that he could pay as well, and Cash was looking for a bigger share of the profits from his hits. Moreover, the producer continued to resist Cash's desire to record gospel material. Equally frustrating was the fact that Phillips to that point had produced only singles, not albums. Though Cash prevailed upon Phillips to let him record an album, the eponymous *Johnny Cash,* the label's first, the producer remained more interested in singles, with their shorter production time, lower costs, easier distribution, and more immediate return on investment. Cash, however, as would soon be demonstrated, was interested in the greater artistic freedom that albums would afford him.

As might have been expected, the breakup was bitter. Aware that Cash was being romanced by Columbia, Phillips asked him directly about the rumors, which Cash denied. "I knew when he opened his mouth he was lying," the Sun maestro later said. "The only damn lie that Johnny Cash ever told me that I was aware of. That hurt. That hurt!" Determined to get his money's worth from his star before his contract expired, Phillips ordered him into the studio to lay down material. Cash resented the treatment almost as much as the hokey doo-wop backing vocals Jack Clement, whom Phillips had brought in to produce Cash's sides, added to songs such as "Guess Things Happen That Way." "I hated that sound," he continued to rail almost three decades later, and in the late 1980s he rerecorded many of the marred Sun sides and some similarly overproduced Columbia material, giving it a more quintessentially spare, lonesome Johnny Cash sound. Phillips would continue recycling and releasing his backlog of Cash material for years after the singer's departure.

Cash's switch to Columbia represented more than a change of labels; it constituted a change of life. Hoping to use his success as a singer as a springboard into television and movie acting, Cash moved himself and his family (by the early 1960s he and Vivian would have four daughters: Roseanne, Kathleen, Cindy, and Tara) to California in 1959. Initially they lived in Encino, in Johnny Carson's former home, but in 1961 Cash purchased 15 acres on a hillside outside Las Casitas, a small town in the rural northern part of the state, and built a sprawling ranch house on it. The area was home to many transplanted southerners, Okies, Arkies, and Texans who had migrated there during and since the Great Depression; though Cash had traveled a different road to get there, he had arrived at the same destination as many of those who shared his background. And, like so many of them, he would discover that California was not the promised land.

Though he had begun using amphetamines in 1957 in Memphis, as a means of staying awake on the long all-night trips from gig to gig, his use of the pills escalated in California and quickly grew into an all-consuming dependence. Initially he rationalized their consumption as a tool for overcoming his inherent shyness, which caused stage fright, and as a necessity for meeting yearly obligations that included close to 300 concert dates as well as the recording sessions to produce several albums. In a very short time, however, it became clear that their use was counterproductive, and Cash was forced to admit that other factors were at play.

"Pills made me feel good," he later simply admitted to Christopher Wren. "I think it was the miserable streak in me. Maybe I was afraid to face reality. Maybe I was trying to find a spiritual satisfaction in drugs. It was an escape, that's all." He had by now essentially abandoned his religious practices, and the restlessness and deep-rooted sorrow that others had always detected in him had grown even more pronounced. Some tried to attribute it to grief over the death of a friend, fellow singer Johnny Horton, who was killed in an automobile accident in 1960, but Cash himself dismissed such speculation. "I acted like it upset me," he told Wren, "but it didn't really. I acted weird about his death, but it was the pills I was on that made me act weird." Others suggested that he was experiencing the loss of equilibrium that often accompanies sudden success and fame, but he did not place much stock in that either, preferring a more straightforward explanation: "When I first started, pills made me feel good. Every time I took them, I felt good. Then I took so many that I just didn't feel good. I was awake, that's all."

Along with the addiction to amphetamines came a corresponding dependence on barbiturates as well as frequent and excessive indulgence in alcohol. He grew moody and unpredictable; exacerbated by uppers, his characteristic nervousness became pathological. Friends remember him literally not being able to sit in a chair for more than a few seconds at a time. He would

In the late 1950s and early 1960s, Cash grew temperamental and unpredictable, partly because of his addiction to amphetamines and dependence on barbiturates and alcohol. He would drive or wander for hours at night by himself when not on tour.

stay up for days on end writing songs, only to discover, when examining his work after a few hours of sleep, that the words made no sense at all. When not on tour he would drive for hours at night by himself off the roads through the Mojave Desert; other times he would enrage his neighbors by placing huge amplifiers on the roof of his house, which already bore a 10-foot electrified cross, and blasting music down into the valley below.

"My friends made a joke about my 'nervousness,'" he wrote in *The Man in Black*. "I had a twitch in the neck, the back, the face. My eyes dilated. I couldn't stand still. I twisted, turned, contorted, and popped my neck bones. It often felt like someone had a fist between my shoulder blades, twisting the muscle and bone, stretching my nerves, torturing them to the breaking point." A penchant for juvenile but essentially harmless pranks while on the road, usually involving cap guns or firecrackers, graduated into genuine destructiveness, with trashed hotel rooms and televisions the norm. Some hotels refused to allow him and his band to stay there, and a series of increasingly darker Johnny Cash stories, often involving weapons and destruction, made the rounds in the industry. There were cancellations of recording sessions and concerts, a few at first and then, in his own words, "nine out of ten recording sessions" and "whole tours." As the amphetamines, drinking, and cigarettes left him with chronic laryngitis, some of the dates he did make were so disastrous as to make him and his audience wish he had stayed home.

For his debut at New York City's prestigious Carnegie Hall in May 1962, he inexplicably took the stage dressed as Jimmie Rodgers, the revered "Singing Brakeman," wearing a railroad man's cap and jacket and swinging Rodgers's own lantern, which he had borrowed from Rodgers's daughter. To the audience's great bewilderment, he sang—or rather, in his own words, as his voice was totally gone, "whispered"—only Rodgers's songs and none of his own material. Country music's first superstar, Rodgers had died of tuberculosis in 1933 at the age of 35, and fans and friends began to wonder if a similarly premature end was not in store for Cash.

A 1965 date at the Ryman Auditorium, where the "Grand Ole Opry" program was broadcast, was even more catastrophic. Cash's "nervousness" often now manifested itself onstage in a constant adjustment of the microphones; when, in the middle of a song, he was unable to remove the mike on the Opry stage from its stand, he kicked it over and then dragged it along the lip of the stage, intentionally shattering 50 or 60 footlights and sending exploding glass shattering all over himself and the audience. Such antics did not go over well at the decorous Opry, and Cash was told never to return. Driving the streets of Nashville later that night, drug-addled and blinded by tears, he crashed the car into a tree and woke up in the hospital with a broken nose and a broken jaw.

Now the name Hank Williams began to be mentioned in connection with Cash; the greatest performer in the history of country music had himself been permanently banned from the Opry stage just four months before his death, caused by addiction to barbiturates and amphetamines, at the age of 29 on New Year's Day, 1953. Before finally getting straight in 1967, Cash would survive several such motor vehicle accidents, waste away to 140 pounds on his six-foot-two-inch frame, live through a couple of overdoses (Marshall Grant had to perform artificial respiration on him on one occasion), accidentally burn down 508 acres of national forest in California, be arrested seven times, and bring about the end of his marriage through his self-described "trashy" living. "I wrecked every car, every truck, every jeep I ever drove during that seven years," he told interviewer Robert

Hilburn in 1973. "I counted the broken bones in my body once. I think I have seventeen."

Miraculously, Cash also managed during that time to produce a large body of vital and important music. On many nights the palpable aura of danger around him seemed only to add to his charisma, and for every disaster like Carnegie Hall there were a dozen scintillating performances, the air of self-destruction only adding to the conviction of the music. To one young concertgoer who saw him live for the first time during these years, the gaunt, emaciated Cash "looked like Abe Lincoln. He looked like the center of the world." A veteran promoter, alarmed at the deterioration in Cash's physical appearance, ordered that only soft spotlights be used during his show but admitted afterward, "he could still make the hair stand up on your arm, and that's what makes 'em buy tickets." The afternoon of the morning that Grant found Cash unconscious and not breathing, "he went on and did a damn good show," the bassist recalled years later in wonder. "He was always capable of that."

A similar mixture of chaos and brilliance prevailed in the studio. His new producer, Don Law, found him to be "a very complex and very tormented person"; like Phillips, Law believed that bringing out the undefinable essence of Cash's voice—even more than the material being sung—was the key to any session with him. "It's the virility and guts to his voice that he's got. He's always sung off pitch, but he can just walk out and say, 'Hello, I'm Johnny Cash.'" He really did not even need a producer, Law came to believe: "There's only one way to record Cash. You get him healthy and you let him go. I knew he was a great talent. I believed in him. Sometimes he couldn't sing a lick, but I knew he had it and I tried to get it out of him." That process of getting it out could sometimes be excruciating. Kris Kristofferson, then an aspiring songwriter who worked as a gofer in the Nashville studios where Cash did most of his recordings, used to sneak in to watch the sessions. "It would be painful," he recalled to Christopher Wren. "John would come in and four hours would go by and nothing would happen. He was wasted, but electric to watch."

Such difficulties were rarely evident on the finished product. Cash's first six singles for Columbia—the lovelorn "What Do I Care" and "All Over Again"; "Frankie's Man, Johnny," a humorous reworking of a traditional tale of love and murder; "Tennessee Flat Top Box," a tribute to Luther Perkins's pristine picking; the first of many gunfighting songs, "Don't Take Your Guns to Town"; and the autobiographical "Five Feet High and Rising," about the Dyess flood—all placed in the top twenty in the national country charts, while the resigned "I Still Miss Someone" was as haunting as anything he would ever record. Though he would later downplay the satisfaction they gave him, perhaps because, as he wrote in *The Man in Black*, "the importance of a hymn album was minimized by so many in the record business that it had lost some of its importance to me," and perhaps because his way of life at the time was at such odds with the sentiments and spirit of the music, he at long last recorded two albums of gospel music, *Hymns by Johnny Cash*, which was released in 1959, and *Hymns from the Heart*, which appeared in 1961.

Other secular hits followed—"I Got Stripes," a somewhat lighthearted prison song; "The Rebel—Johnny Yuma," a theme for the television show of the same name; the perennial bluegrass favorite "The Orange Blossom Special"; and two straight number ones, "Ring of Fire," a mariachi-flavored declaration of the consuming powers of love, and "Understand Your Man." In 1967, as his marriage was officially ending, the sizzling "Jackson" reached number two in the charts; a duet with his longtime backup singer, June Carter of the acclaimed Carter family, the song amounted to a virtual public declaration of their love for each other and won for them that year's Grammy Award for best country and western performance by a duet, trio, or group. Several moodier, more powerful pieces—"Dark as a Dungeon," the Merle Travis classic about life as a coal miner; "Long Black Veil," a tale of murder and betrayal narrated by the ghost of a hanged man; and "The Wall" and "25 Minutes to Go," two more prison songs, the last narrated by a man awaiting his execution—displayed Cash's continuing commitment to painting pictures from life's other side.

In fact Cash's most committed, passionate music from this period was essentially noncommercial, recorded for four remarkable concept albums—*Ride This Train,* released in 1960; *Blood, Sweat and Tears,* released in 1962; *Bitter Tears,* released in 1964; and *Ballads of the True West,* released in 1965—that revealed his broad vision of country music as a living repository of American history and lore as well as an evolving modern genre capable of addressing the most topical issues. The term *concept album,* meaning a collection of songs or musical pieces relating to a unifying central theme, motif, or narrative, would

come to be associated with such rock groups as the Beatles, the Who, Jethro Tull, and Pink Floyd, but it was Cash who got there first, using folk material and original contemporary compositions both to celebrate and preserve the rich heritage and diversity of a largely bygone America and to protest past and continued injustices.

Ride This Train, which Cash called a "country opera," reflects his (and country music's) continued obsession with the railroad. Connected by Cash's evocative narrative spoken over the sound of a steam locomotive, the album's 10 songs function as a musical travelogue that

June Carter and her mother, Maybelle Carter (of the famed Carter Family), perform with Johnny Cash in 1977. Ten years earlier, Johnny and June won a Grammy award for their duet "Jackson," which was nearly a public declaration of their love for each other.

celebrates the land itself and reminds the listener of forgotten day-to-day episodes of American history as lived by the common people—settlers and farmers, miners, itinerant laborers, lumberjacks, trappers, hunters, migrant workers, cowhands, slaves, and outlaws—whose struggles, small triumphs, and heartbreaks, experienced in search of freedom and dignity, forged the national character.

Blood, Sweat and Tears explores similar themes, exalting, in Bob Allen's words, "the toil, sacrifice, risk, and hard-fought pride of the millions of faceless workers—indentured servants, slaves, convicts, railroad work gangs, free blacks, and others—on whose backs and 'blood, sweat and tears' the U.S. economy was born." The by-now-familiar Cash characters appear: convicts on the chain gang, railroad workers, miners, drifters, sharecroppers, and even the legendary engineer Casey Jones, with Cash celebrating the restless independence and pride of each. The centerpiece of the album is a stirring eight-minute rendition of the timeless folk ballad "John Henry," the legendary "steel-driving man" of the railroad, who died with his "hammer in his hand" after outracing a steam drill to demonstrate the indomitability of the human spirit. In the spirit of the song's hero, Cash accompanied himself in the studio while recording the song by banging together two eight-pound bars of steel; when the recording was finished, his hands were bleeding and raw. According to Don Law, such immersion in the subject matter was typical of Cash's passionate approach to his concept material, which required a great deal of musical and historical research. "He had an unquenchable desire for knowledge," Law said. "He soaked up everything he needed to know, and no matter what state he was in, he could pull a project together."

Such commitment was also in evidence on *Ballads of the True West,* a collection of mostly folk songs put together by Cash to tell the story of the white settlement of the frontier, from the first sighting by Native Americans of the boats bringing the Europeans to their shores. Country musicians and their audience had long identified with cowboys and the conquest of the West—Hank Williams, for example, named his backing band the Drifting Cowboys, and innumerable country musicians affected western attire—for the same reason that they preferred the term "country and western" to the somewhat pejorative "hillbilly": because such a heritage seemed more glamorous and romantic than that of a rural southerner. On Cash's Western album, however, the bloodshed, waste, and hardship of western life does much to deglamorize the myth, although there is no doubt that he also finds a great deal of heroism in the sagas of those who settled the western lands. By his own account he did an immense amount of research into the subject, in the form of both reading and attempts to relive the western experience: "I followed trails in my jeep and on foot, and I slept under mesquite bushes and in gullies. I heard the timber wolves, looked for golden nuggets in creek beds, sat for hours beneath a manzanita bush in an ancient Indian burial ground, breathed the West wind and heard the tales it tells only to those who listen. I replaced a wooden grave marker of some man in Arizona who never made it. I walked across alkali flats where others had walked before me, but hadn't made it."

That Cash was aware of the dark side of the western legend was made abundantly clear by *Bitter Tears,* the most powerful and the most controversial of his concept albums and one that he considers to be quite possibly his best work. It was born of his increased immersion in the so-called folk music revival of the 1960s and of his intense friendship with the leading talent to emerge from that movement, Bob Dylan. Initially, of course, no distinction could be made between folk and country music—

indeed, the two terms were synonymous—but during the Great Depression, the fascination of liberal northern political activists with the union and labor ballads of Kentucky coal miners and Carolina mill workers, and especially with the topical and Dust Bowl ballads of Woody Guthrie, led to a perceived divergence of category. By the early 1960s the term "folk music" was still used to refer to traditional, noncommercial music that had been passed on, but it included as well new, topical, often politically oriented material—so-called protest songs—written and performed by musicians such as Dylan, Joan Baez, Pete Seeger, and Peter, Paul, and Mary who considered themselves to be following in Guthrie's footsteps. As in a very short time the new folk music, which was centered in Greenwich Village in New York City, became inextricably linked with northern liberal support of the black civil rights movement in the South, many of its practitioners and devotees were eager to dissociate it from its roots in country, which as the music of white rural southerners was seen as inherently racist and representative of the culture of oppression in the South. The "purists" of the new folk movement, who performed only to the accompaniment of acoustic, unamplified instruments, also considered rock and roll anathema, viewing it as a purely commercial product with no political or social content. Needless to say, most of the country music audience wanted little to do with the new folk music either.

But Cash had never been bound by such categorizing, as his Sun work had shown, and much of the material on his concept albums could have fit into the repertoire of any of the new "folkies." He and Dylan shared similar musical roots, as well as the recognition that the music they loved sprang from common ground. Infatuated with a romanticized notion of the depression-era railriding hobo myths that Ray Cash had actually experienced,

Twenty-two-year-old Bob Dylan sings his "Blowin' in the Wind" to folk music fans in 1963. Cash admired Dylan's work, and once said Dylan "was one of the best country singers I had ever heard."

Dylan had first arrived in New York City as a lad of 19 in early 1961, after hitchhiking from his home in Minnesota to visit his dying idol, Woody Guthrie, in his New Jersey hospital. But his first musical hero had been Hank Williams, and it was Elvis who had first showed him the direction his life would take. "When I first heard Elvis's voice," Dylan remembered in 1987,

"I just knew that I wasn't going to work for anybody and nobody was gonna be my boss. Hearing him for the first time was like busting out of jail."

Surprisingly, the fledgling singer-songwriter's work had a similarly strong effect on Cash. After just six months in New York, Dylan had been signed by Columbia, but when his first album sold only a few hundred copies, many at the label wanted to drop him. Cash intervened, letting everybody at Columbia know, in the words of John Hammond, the legendary executive who brought Dylan to the label, that "he thought Dylan was a giant. There's no higher recommendation possible." At that point the two had not yet met. "He had his first record out when I discovered him," Cash recalled in 1969. "I was working joints in downtown Las Vegas, the Nugget and places like that, and I was staying up all night playing Bob Dylan after I got through." He began writing to Dylan, whose replies constitute some of his most treasured possessions: "I never have showed those letters to anyone, even June. . . . I have probably a dozen or more locked in my vault. I would never let those letters out of my vault." Dylan's second album, *The Freewheelin' Bob Dylan,* which contained the classic "Blowin' in the Wind" as well as several protest songs about the civil rights movement, impressed Cash even more. "I thought he was one of the best country singers I had ever heard," said Cash, using his typically catholic definition of country music.

The two began hanging out together in Greenwich Village when Cash was in New York. Through Dylan, Cash met Peter LaFarge, a fellow singer and songwriter, full-blooded Nargaset Indian, former rodeo cowboy, and stepson of the Native American writer Oliver LaFarge, whose novel *Laughing Boy* had won the Pulitzer Prize for fiction in 1930. At a Village coffeehouse one night in 1963, Cash heard LaFarge sing a stunning original composition about a Native American named Ira Hayes, a member of the dispossessed Pima tribe and a decorated World War II hero—he was one of the marines shown in the famous photograph raising the U.S. flag during the bitter battle for the Pacific Ocean atoll of Iwo Jima—who nevertheless died poor, drunk, and dishonored in two inches of water in a ditch, "alone in the land he'd fought to save." Cash hurried into the studio to record it as his next single; it was released in the summer of 1964, followed in October by *Bitter Tears,* a collection of LaFarge's and his own songs about the historical injustices suffered by Native Americans.

"I just felt the American Indian had suffered great injustices through the treaties that were broken," Cash said in explaining his motivation for making his album of what LaFarge called "Indian freedom songs," but the reaction of the country music establishment was outrage. Upset by its content, many country disc jockeys were reluctant to play "The Ballad of Ira Hayes" when it was released. Their anger only increased when Cash made a triumphant appearance in July 1964 at the Newport Folk Festival, where he cemented his friendship with Dylan— the two exchanged guitars—and stunned the crowd with a set that included "Ira Hayes," Dylan's "Don't Think Twice, It's All Right," and "I Walk the Line." When the blacklist of "Ira Hayes" then intensified, Cash took out a full-page advertisement in *Billboard,* the music industry's most important journal, in which he charged radio programmers with cowardice and implicitly linked the concept of Native American rights with other controversial issues in American life—specifically, the poverty in black urban ghettos, the civil rights movement, and the war in Vietnam. Predictably, Cash only aroused further ire, with the editor of one prominent country magazine calling upon him to resign from the Country Music Association (CMA) because "you and your crowd are just too intelligent to associate with plain country folks, country artists, and country deejays" and the Ku Klux Klan mobilizing a hate campaign against him. When *Bitter Tears* was released, *Billboard* refused to review it and Columbia did little to promote it.

Though nasty, the flap did not greatly damage Cash's career, for by now he was well enough established as an artist to walk his own line. The only one capable of destroying Johnny Cash's career was himself, a realization he reached in November 1967 when he went cold turkey to kick pills. His determination to succeed in that endeavor had been strengthened by the deepening over the years of his relationship with June Carter, and the two were married on March 1, 1968, two months after his divorce from Vivian Liberto became final. The marriage to Carter gave him a living link to country music history; June's mother, Maybelle Carter, had been, with her cousin Sara and Sara's husband, A. P. Carter, one of the members of the original Carter Family, who with Jimmie Rodgers had been the most successful and influential early country music act. (The modern incarnation of the Carter Family—Maybelle, June, and June's sisters Helen and Anita—had been a familiar part of Johnny Cash concerts since 1961, along with the Statler Brothers, a popular vocal group, and Carl Perkins. The original Tennessee Three—Grant, Luther Perkins, and a drummer, W. S. Holland, who made the duo a trio starting in 1960—continued to back Cash on the road and sometimes in the studio until 1968, when Perkins was killed in a fire in his home.)

Along with his marriage to June Carter and his return to health, Cash experienced a spiritual rebirth, presided over by the Reverend Jimmie Rodgers Snow, son of Hank Snow, the famed "Singing Ranger," who had been one of the Grand Ole Opry's greatest stars. He moved back to Tennessee, to a striking wooden lakefront home in Hen-

dersonville, not far from Nashville, and the country music establishment embraced him as enthusiastically as had the congregation a repentant sinner in the churches of his youth.

He still went his own way, of course, but now more than ever he was able to make others follow; the Man in Black had been born. His live prison albums, *Johnny Cash at Folsom Prison* and *Johnny Cash at San Quentin,* released in 1968 and 1969, both went to the top of the charts and yielded number one singles—"Folsom Prison Blues" and "A Boy Named Sue," one of the many comic numbers that Cash would release over the succeeding years. Being born again had cost him none of his edge, though; the *Folsom* album contained another unrepentant killer in the person of the narrator of "Cocaine Blues," and Cash's performance of the bitterly scathing "San Quentin" left

In 1969 Johnny Cash and the Tennessee Three entertain inmates at Folsom Prison in California. Cash's live performances in prisons were frowned upon by many in the music establishment; however, "Folsom Prison Blues" won Cash a Grammy award for best male vocal in 1968.

his audience of convicts in such a frenzy that the guards feared they were going to riot. "The guards were scared to death," said Cash. "All the convicts were standing up on the dining tables. They were out of control, really. During the second rendition of that song, all I would have had to do was say, 'Break!' and they were gone, man. They were ready! . . . I knew I had that prison audience where all I had to do was say, 'Take over!' and they would have. The guards knew it, too. I was tempted."

Though *Rolling Stone* magazine interpreted the prison albums as an indication of his solidarity with the counterculture—"Singing inside a prison to men whose spirits are being destroyed is Johnny Cash's kind of revolution; where must Cash be *at* to relate so well to those we have put inside our dungeons?"—he won a Grammy award for best male vocal performance for "Folsom Prison Blues" and for best album notes for *Johnny Cash at Folsom Prison* in 1968, and an unprecedented five CMA awards the next year for the *San Quentin* album. In 1970 he won two Grammys, for best male vocalist and for best liner notes, for an admiring poem about Bob Dylan he had contributed to that artist's *Nashville Skyline* album. That same year Cash's recording of Kris Kristofferson's "Sunday Morning Comin' Down" won that songwriter the CMA's award for best song of the year. Bill Malone called the appearance of the unkempt, bearded, seemingly stoned Kristofferson at the award ceremonies a "turning point" in country music history; if it seemed to many that the freaks and

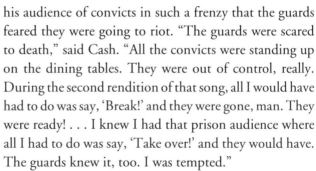

Ray Charles joins Cash in a song on "The Johnny Cash Show" in 1970. Cash became the first country artist to be given a weekly TV program, and he brought to it an exceptional variety of musicians—Arlo Guthrie, Pete Seeger, Bob Dylan, Mahalia Jackson, and Merle Haggard, among others.

hippies had at that moment at last succeeded in overrun-
ning Nashville, there was now no turning back. Kristofferson's entrée, made possible by Cash, paved the way for
the overdue success in the 1970s of such longhaired
country "outlaws"—"hippie rednecks" others called
them—as Willie Nelson and Waylon Jennings (with
whom Cash had lived briefly during the craziest of his
drug days). Cash's exact position on the social issues of
the day was always somewhat difficult to divine, however,
implied more than directly stated; if songs like "What Is
Truth?" and "The Man in Black" seemed to express
sympathy for youthful protest and skepticism about
American involvement in Vietnam, Cash also played
for the troops there, performed at the Nixon White
House (where, however, he
played "What Is Truth?"), and
announced his belief that all
Americans should get behind
the president.

On March 10, 1976,
Cash and his wife, June,
and their son, John, pose
beside the Walk of Fame
star honoring Johnny in
Hollywood, California.
The star tribute is generally
reserved for those who are
perceived as being at the
top of the entertainment
field.

In 1969, at the height of this
success, Cash was given a weekly one-hour network television
program. The first country artist
to achieve such a distinction, he
succeeded in bringing an unprecedented array of diverse musical talent to the stage of the
Ryman Auditorium, where the
show was filmed—Bob Dylan,
the Who, Louis Armstrong,
Neil Young, Pete Seeger, Joni
Mitchell, Ray Charles, and Mahalia Jackson, among others. He
took special delight in having
Merle Haggard on the show;
Haggard, who had been in the

Actor Kirk Douglas (left), writer Hal Bloom, and Johnny and his wife, June, take a break while on the set of the movie *A Gunfight* in 1970. The film, shot in New Mexico, is about two famous gunfighters, played by Douglas and Cash, who stage a duel for money.

audience as an inmate at Cash's first San Quentin concert back in 1958, had also been banned by the Grand Ole Opry for his outrageous conduct on its stage.

"The Johnny Cash Show" ran for two seasons. Its cancellation in 1971 indeed indicated a slight waning in Cash's popularity; the creator of five number one hits between 1968 and 1970 would not have another record top the charts until 1976—the humorous "One Piece at a Time," about a Detroit automobile plant worker who builds a unique patchwork car out of parts he smuggles out of his job over many years—and none as a solo artist thereafter.

He continued, however, to work prolifically. Included among his releases were three more concept albums—

From Sea to Shining Sea, the patriotic *America,* and the reflective *The Rambler*—and, as an indication of his renewal of his early vow to "tithe" a portion of his music, several religious albums, including one, *Johnny Cash in the Holy Land,* recorded in Israel. (He also made a religious film in Israel, *Gospel Road,* about the life of Jesus.) In the meantime his secular music of the late 1970s onward demonstrated a continued commitment to recording material from outside the country mainstream, most notably compositions by Mick Jagger and Keith Richards ("No Expectations") and Bruce Springsteen ("Highway Patrolman"). In 1979 he employed British new waver Nick Lowe, the husband of his stepdaughter Carleen Carter, as his producer, but their collaboration failed to match the artistic level of Cash's best work and did not perform well commercially—a harbinger of a disturbing trend, for in 1982 a remarkable streak of 26 years with at least one single on the country charts came to an end. Three years later Columbia unceremoniously dropped him from the label, a move that elicited howls of outrage and that one music journalist likened to dynamiting Mount Rushmore.

For Cash, Columbia's decision was not necessarily a tragedy. He was more than financially secure and seemingly had little left to prove. Election to the Country Music Hall of Fame had come in 1980—at the age of 48, he was the youngest inductee ever—and induction to the Rock and Roll Hall of Fame would come in 1991. His music was, and is, in no danger of being forgotten: a generation of new artists, everyone from punk rockers Social Distortion to megaband U2, has cited him as an inspiration; his daughter Roseanne has established herself as a superb songwriter and singer who is certain to maintain the family tradition (she even scored a number one country hit with one of his songs from the Sun years, "Tennessee Flat Top Box"); and the best of his work is still readily available. He could justifiably ease into stately semiretirement, as befitting a national monument in his sixties with occasional health problems (he endured a brief stay at the Betty Ford Clinic for dependence on prescription medication in 1984, and heart bypass surgery in 1988). Or he could rouse himself for the occasional gig, add to his long list of television and movie

credits, (in which he has most often been cast as a gunfighter or killer), update his autobiography (which was published by Zondervan in 1975), write novels (his first, *Man in White*, an account of the conversion of Paul, was published in 1986), or simply stay at home in Hendersonville with June and their son, John Carter Cash, who was born on March 3, 1970. But instead he carries

The Highwaymen—(left to right) Willie Nelson, Johnny Cash, Waylon Jennings, and Kris Kristofferson—perform a benefit concert in New York's Central Park in May 1993.

On January 16, 1991, Cash proudly raises his award in the air after his induction into the Rock and Roll Hall of Fame in New York.

on, the Man in Black wandering eternally from town to town, singing his sad, stoic, lonesome, and celebratory songs, still playing upward of 100 dates a year to audiences that range from tens of thousands of fans at the annual Farm Aid concerts to just several hundred at his wildly anticipated yearly club gigs in New York City, even returning to the top of the charts periodically as one of the Highwaymen, a country music supergroup composed of him, Kris Kristofferson, Waylon Jennings, and Willie

Nelson. "To see and hear Johnny Cash perform today," wrote Arthur Levy in 1991, "is to experience rock 'n' roll survival at the hands of a true caretaker."

Restless as ever and true to his roots, Cash is not content just looking after the grounds; he has more seeds to plant and make grow. In 1994 a new album, *American Recordings*, is to be released on American. His unlikely presence on that hip label of rappers and heavy metalers is itself testimony to his eternal appeal. He has written most of the songs on the album, including "Delia's Gone," "Let the Train Blow the Whistle," and "Like a Soldier." "I just don't hear any great new song stylists," he said in 1993, commenting on today's dearth of American songwriters. "No Kris Kristofferson. No Bob Dylan. There'll never be another Bob Dylan, of course, but I don't see anyone who gets out and does it their own damn way and damn the torpedoes. . . . I want to hear people who don't care what's selling now but say this is the way I want to do it."

Perhaps he is asking too much. For Cash's old Sun colleague Jerry Lee Lewis, the highest compliment a singer can receive is to be called a stylist, a term he reserves for the very few vocalists who can take any song and make it, through the sheer force of their distinctive musical personality, forever and exclusively their own. For the stylist, the artificial categories of music simply do not exist: The singer is more important than the song, and there is no such thing as rock and roll music, or country music, or rockabilly, or folk; there is only Jerry Lee Lewis music, or Johnny Cash music. Johnny Cash, said Jerry Lee way back when, is clearly such a stylist; and who could you expect to make Johnny Cash music but Johnny Cash? "They can take all the synthesizers they want," Cash once said when asked whether his music could stand up against more contemporary sounds, "but nothing will take the place of the human heart."

Selected Discography ★ ★ ★ ★ ★ ★ ★ ★ ★ ★ ★ ★

(Editor's note: Many of Cash's original recordings are now out of print. However, virtually all of his most important work is available on various reissues and anthology collections.)

Johnny Cash: The Sun Years. Rhino Records, 1990. (14 of the Sun sides.)

The Essential Johnny Cash, 1955–1983. Columbia, 1992. (An anthology of 75 Cash recordings, covering mostly the years with Columbia but including as well 15 of the most important Sun sides.)

Johnny Cash: The Gospel Collection. Columbia, 1992. (The two gospel albums Cash recorded for Columbia in 1959 and 1961, *Hymns by Johnny Cash* and *Hymns from the heart.)*

Classic Cash. Mercury, 1988. (Cash's rerecorded versions of many of his best-known songs from the Sun and Columbia years.)

Johnny Cash at Folsom Prison and San Quentin. Columbia, 1989. (The two legendary prison-concert albums combined in one set.)

The Man in Black, 1954–1959. Bear Family, 1990. (All of the Sun and early Columbia material from those years, including studio outtakes and unreleased material.)

The Man in Black, 1959–1962. Bear Family, 1991. (All of the Columbia material from those years, including studio outtakes and unreleased material.)

Come Along and Ride This Train. Bear Family, 1991. (All seven of the concept albums Cash recorded between 1960 and 1977: *Ride This Train; Blood, Sweat and Tears; Bitter Tears; Ballads of the True West; From Sea to Shining Sea; America;* and *The Rambler.)*

American Recordings. American, 1994. (Thirteen songs recorded in album producer Rick Rubin's living room and at Johnny's cabin, except the songs "Tennessee Stud" and "The Man Who Couldn't Cry," which were recorded live at the Hollywood nightclub The Viper Room.)

Further Reading ★ ★ ★ ★ ★ ★ ★ ★ ★ ★ ★ ★ ★ ★

Cash, Johnny. *The Man in Black.* Grand Rapids: Zondervan, 1975.

————. *The Man in White.* San Francisco: Harper, 1986.

————. *The Songs of Johnny Cash.* New York: Dial, 1970.

de Bedts, Ralph F. *Recent American History: 1933 Through World War II.* Homewood, IL: Dorsey Press, 1973.

Escott, Colin, with Martin Hawkins. *Good Rockin' Tonight: Sun Records and the Birth of Rock 'n' Roll.* New York: St. Martin's, 1991.

Flippo, Chet. *Your Cheatin' Heart: A Biography of Hank Williams.* Garden City, NY: Doubleday, 1985.

McElvaine, Robert S. *The Great Depression: America, 1929–1941.* New York: Times Books, 1984.

Malone, Bill C. *Country Music U.S.A.* Austin: University of Texas, 1985.

The Rolling Stone Interviews: 1967–1980. New York: St. Martin's, 1981.

Scaduto, Anthony. *Bob Dylan: An Intimate Biography.* New York: Grosset & Dunlap, 1971.

Shelton, Robert. *No Direction Home: The Life and Music of Bob Dylan.* New York: Morrow, 1986.

Wren, Christopher S. *Winners Got Scars Too: The Life and Legends of Johnny Cash.* New York: Dial, 1971.

Chronology ★ ★ ★ ★ ★ ★ ★ ★ ★ ★ ★ ★ ★ ★ ★ ★ ★

1932	Born J. R. Cash on February 26, in Kingsland, Arkansas.
1935	Ray Cash and his family becomes part of a FERA colonization project and is transported to Dyess, Arkansas
1937	In January the Cash family is forced to evacuate their home because of floods; the Cashes return about a month later
1944	J. R.'s beloved brother Jack dies in May after an accident.
1950	J. R. graduates from high school; enlists in the U.S. Air Force where he begins to use the name John and serves as a radio operator
1954	Cash is honorably discharged from the air force after attaining the rank of staff sergeant; Sam Phillips records Elvis Presley on the Sun label; Cash marries Vivian Liberto on August 7 and they later settle in Memphis, Tennessee
1955	First of the Cashes' four daughters, Roseanne, is born in May; Johnny's first Sun record, "Cry, Cry, Cry" backed with "Hey, Porter," is released in June and reaches top of Memphis country charts
1956	"I Walk the Line," Cash's first crossover hit, is released in April
1957	First album, *Johnny Cash,* is released; Cash signs with Columbia Records
1959	Cash moves his family to Encino, California; records his first gospel album, *Hymns by Johnny Cash*
1960	Records *Ride This Train,* the first of his self-described "country operas"
1962	Burdened by a deepening dependence on alcohol and drugs, he gives a disastrous performance at New York City's Carnegie Hall in May
1963	Charts two number one hits, "Ring of Fire" and "Understand Your Man"
1964	Performs with Bob Dylan at the Newport Folk Festival in July; *Bitter Tears,* a collection of songs about injustices against Native Americans, is released in October

★ ★

1967	Cash kicks his drug addiction; his marriage to Vivian ends; records number one single, "Jackson," with June Carter
1968	Marries June Carter on March 1; experiences spiritual rebirth; moves to Hendersonville, Tennessee; live prison album *Johnny Cash at Folsom Prison* is released; wins Grammy award for "Folsom Prison Blues"
1969	Records *Johnny Cash at San Quentin*; debuts weekly one-hour television program, "The Johnny Cash Show"
1970	Only son, John Carter Cash, is born on March 3; plays for American troops in Vietnam; wins two more Grammy awards
1971	"Johnny Cash Show" is canceled
1975	Cash's autobiography, *The Man in Black,* is published
1976	Records "One Piece at a Time," his last number one single to date
1977	Releases *The Rambler,* last of his concept albums to date
1980	Cash is elected to the Country Music Hall of Fame
1985	Makes first appearances and recordings as one of the Highwaymen, with Willie Nelson, Waylon Jennings, and Kris Kristofferson
1986	Columbia drops Cash from the label; Cash wins Grammy award for best country recording for "The Highwayman"; publishes *The Man in White,* a fictionalized account of the conversion of Paul
1988	Undergoes successful heart bypass surgery
1991	Elected to the Rock and Roll Hall of Fame
1992	Featured as guest vocalist on "The Wanderer," cut on Irish rock group U2's smash album *Zooropa*
1994	Comeback album, *American Recordings,* is released

Index ★★★★★★★★★★★★★★★★★★★★★★★★

★ ★

Sean Dolan holds a B.A. degree in literature and American history from SUNY Oswego. He is the author of many biographies and histories for young adult readers, including *James Beckwourth* and *Michael Jordan* in Chelsea House's BLACK AMERICANS OF ACHIEVEMENT series, and has edited a series of volumes on the famous explorers of history. His lifelong interest in the music of Johnny Cash began when his father, a high school social studies teacher concerned with Native American rights, brought home the *Bitter Tears* album.

Leeza Gibbons is a reporter for and cohost of the nationally syndicated television program "Entertainment Tonight" and NBC's daily talk show "John & Leeza from Hollywood." A graduate of the University of South Carolina's School of Journalism, Gibbons joined the on-air staff of "Entertainment Tonight" in 1984 after cohosting WCBS-TV's "Two on the Town" in New York City. Prior to that, she cohosted "PM Magazine" on WFAA-TV in Dallas, Texas, and on KFDM-TV in Beaumont, Texas. Gibbons also hosts the annual "Miss Universe," "Miss U.S.A.," and "Miss Teen U.S.A." pageants, as well as the annual Hollywood Christmas Parade. She is active in a number of charities and has served as the national chairperson for the Spinal Muscular Atrophy Division of the Muscular Dystrophy Association; each September, Gibbons cohosts the National MDA Telethon with Jerry Lewis.